Precious Pearls

An Inheritance of Tears and Treasures

Blessings to you,
Margaret Feaver

Margaret R. Feaver

Precious Pearls
An Inheritance of Tears and Treasures

By Margaret R. Feaver

Except where otherwise indicated, all Scripture quotations in
this book are taken from the Holy Bible, New International
Version. Copyright 1973, 1978, 1984 by the International
Bible Society. Used by permission of Zondervan Bible
Publishers.

International Standard Book Number: 1-928715-31-1

All the stories in this book are true, but a few names and
details have been changed to protect the privacy of the
individuals mentioned.

Library of Congress number 2001098623

Printed in the United States of America.

Dedication

I dedicate this book to my husband, Douglas,
my faithful lifetime partner in love and prayer and
ministry; to our children: David, John, Ruth and
Peter, through whom God has taught us His ways and
the joy of love and laughter; to all our grandchildren
who inspired the writing of this book
that they may pass on their heritage of spiritual
riches to the next generation.

*And in loving memory of our son Paul,
who claimed his heavenly inheritance ahead of us.*

Acknowledgments

Before I get to the long list of those who must be thanked, I want first to honor my missionary parents, Roy and Gertrude Seaman, who by their godly example of dedicated service to Jesus Christ taught me the beauty and value of obedience to God and His Word.

Thank you Douglas, my loving companion and strong support for over 50 years. With your knowledge of Biblical languages, you have held my hand through teaching and writing lest I trip on theological issues. And with your love, you have held me close to your heart.

Thank you dear children — David, John, Ruth and Peter along with your spouses Nan, Gail, David Green and Karen — for contributing so much to the spiritual fabric of our family life. I am blessed beyond measure for the joy of knowing each of you!

Thank you, Katie Kricks, for being my dear friend and faithful prayer partner for years.

Thank you, Carol Brown, wife of Pastor Keith Brown, for standing at my door with a gift of manuscript paper and pens and challenging me to "start writing" this book. Thanks, too, to all the others who continued to give me persistent nudges.

Thank you, Frank and Catherine Ternigan, and Bill and Sally Coleman, our friends and co-leaders in ministry, and to all our friends in the Bethlehem Christian Fellowship for your prayers and loving support which is impossible to measure.

Thank you, Loren and Darlene Cunningham, founders of Youth With A Mission, and Howard Malmstadt, co-founder of the University of the Nations, for opening the door for us to be pioneers in missions in our retirement years.

Thank you, Fay Williams, my dear friend and powerful intercessor, for your prayers and encouragement. Because of your example in writing "The World in Our Hearts," I was challenged to write my own stories.

Thank you, dear Writers Group – Audra Baumgarth, Marge Clewett, Richie Lambeth, Yolanda Olson, Roxanne Olson, Matt Rawlins, Ross Tooley and many others under the excellent leadership of Sandi Tompkins. You have been my cheerleaders, inspiring me to capture these precious pearls of God's wisdom and truth on paper. For six years, we have worked hard together, through laughter and tears. You all have been the highlight of my week.

Thank you, Kathy Fitts, you are a gifted photographer and I appreciate your thoughtful work on the creative concept for the book cover.

Thank you, Scott and Sandi Tompkins. My profound gratitude goes to you not only for your outstanding editing, but for a decade of love and encouragement. You expressed grace and generosity to me in your inestimable gift of sculpting these pages into a book. Without you, my manuscript would still be on the shelf.

Above all, I give thanks to my Lord God, the giver of all good gifts, who gave me these precious pearls of wisdom and truth as an inheritance.

Contents

Testing, Trials and Triumphs

Expanding Ministry

More Lessons

The YWAM Years

INTRODUCTION

Dear Friend,

If I had the choice I would like to invite you to our home for a cup of tea, a time to "talk story" as the Hawaiians say. Our family has always loved to tell stories, and it would be a pleasure to listen to yours, too.

I would like to ask you not only to hear what happened, but see with inner eyes some hidden pearls which God revealed through times of trials and tears. As parents enjoy the charms of innocent children, I hope you will chuckle at the humor of our childish ways and be impressed by the patience of our Heavenly Father.

I have collected a few of my treasures of truth to show you God's faithfulness and love to one who trusts Him. If you are encouraged to make your own collection and to be amazed at God's care for just one of His large family, the purpose of this book has been achieved.

Please get comfortable, sit back and relax while you journey with me through these adventures.

May God richly bless you,

Margaret

TREASURES FROM EARLY TRIALS

Miss Hearn and her friends were breathless from running through the hills, hunted like animals by the gang of angry men. The Chinese guerrillas were out to kill all "foreign devils," including these white-faced Christians. The year was 1900 and this nationwide assault on foreigners was known as the Boxer Rebellion.

Only five years earlier this same woman — my mother's Auntie Hearn – had responded to the prayers and passionate pleas for help by Hudson Taylor, founder of the China Inland Mission. On New Year's Eve, 1895, she obeyed God's call to leave her family in England and join a band of missionaries bound for China. Like the other young, dedicated missionaries in the group, Auntie Hearn knew she was making a long-term commitment. It would be seven to ten years before they would return to visit their homeland again, if ever.

Once in China they dedicated their lives to serving the people, showing by their example the love of the Savior they proclaimed. But good works mattered little to the revolutionaries who wanted to rid China of all foreign influences. Eventually, Auntie Hearn and many others had to flee for their lives. They raced across the hills by night and hid in caves by day.

We know very little about Auntie Hearn's last days and hours. We do know that some Chinese friend apparently found a little book which was passed to leaders in the Mission. Eventually it was put on display in a Christian bookstore window in London. In time it was given to my Mother who passed it on to me.

In the beginning of this precious little book Auntie Hearn wrote, ". . .we should love Him equally in pains and pleasures." Further into the worn pages of this early edition of the well-loved classic *Daily Light*, are handwritten notes in the margins alongside the Scripture texts. They were written during those last terrifying days when Auntie Hearn was fleeing from the Chinese guerillas. Let me quote a few of those notes scribbled in faded ink:

July 21 "Love of God manifested in a special way."

July 22 "Wang came in to escort us to further hiding in the hills."

July 23 "Left early for a deserted place in the hills. . .Very tired after a rush over the hills. Had a night with mosquitoes."

July 24 "God's Word very comforting."

As far as I can tell, those are the last words she wrote. The next two pages are missing. Auntie Hearn was caught and killed. My mother, who served over 30 years as a missionary in China, once told me that she felt God called her to take the place of her Auntie Hearn.

In the devotional book Auntie Hearn also scribbled in a quote from Brother Lawrence: "We must know God before we can love; in order to know God, we must often think of Him; and when we come to love Him, we shall then also think of Him often, for our heart will be with our treasure." She then added her own comment: "Let all our employment be to know God: the more one knows Him the more one desires to know Him, and as knowledge is commonly measured of love, the deeper and more extensive our knowledge shall be, the greater will be our love..."

I like to describe this obedience to God's call as our missionary heritage which has been passed down from generation to generation in this last century. There will not be much in the way of wealth and possessions for me to give our family as a material inheritance, but I have a great treasure of spiritual riches to share. This *Daily Light* is one of my greatest treasures — a symbol of a martyr who laid down her life for Jesus, like those heroes and heroines of faith, "of whom the world was not worthy," portrayed in Hebrews 11:38 (KJV).

We may not be asked to die as martyrs, but we are all asked to lay down our lives for Jesus. Simply put, that means to give Him those choices in our lives which we like to control. It means spending our lives no longer in self-centered pursuits, but seeking to please Him. Those who do, have discovered God's secrets. You may not inherit a pot of gold, but a clay pot filled with God's treasures.

CHILDHOOD SEPARATIONS IN CHINA

My mother came from England and my father from Australia, and they met as missionaries in China. After marriage they continued their work there, and my two sisters and I were born in inland China. One of my earliest and most emotional memories of China is the farewell my sister Doris and I faced when sent away to a British missionary boarding school in the port city of Chefoo.

I was six years old at the time, and Doris was a year younger. I believe my parents thought it would be easier for us to go together rather than for me to go alone, but leaving home at such an early age was painful for me and particularly difficult for my sister.

We lived in a self-contained compound surrounded by a high wall with five gates. About 300 of us lived in this beautiful area which included schools, family houses, a hospital, a business store, a guest home and a Memorial Hall for community services and other functions.

After the familiarity of our home life, the school's strict routine seemed cold and foreign. We woke up to a gong ringing at 6:10 a.m. and the rest of the day we lived by bells: a bell to line up, a bell to start class, a bell to move forward. We all knew what the bells signaled. After dressing in the morning a bell would ring to start our 20-minute

Quiet Time and another bell to close it. We had a similar set of bedtime bells including our 15 minutes Quiet Time on our knees. If we were late in line-up or were talking when we should be silent or left clothes items in wrong places, we earned "black marks."

At the end of each month our bad marks were tallied and if they reached a given limit, we lost the privilege of joining our peers on the monthly school outing. This meant staying at school while all our friends went on a picnic to the cherry orchards, the hills, beach or Lighthouse Island. Two months in a row, I missed the monthly holiday and had to stay behind and memorize French verbs because I had left coats or shoes, gloves or whatever outside the assigned closets. My two sisters and I had grown up with servants so we hadn't learned how to keep house, and we came to think such chores were beneath us. Now the shame of public listing and the disappointment of missing out on the fun was causing me to re-think my attitudes.

The teachers apparently decided I needed some T.L.C. (Tender Loving Care) rather than punishment and put me in the infirmary for a weekend of rest. That seemed to break the pattern and I continued to enjoy school and do well. To help motivate our efforts toward excellence, the school was divided into three competing Houses: Amy Carmichael, Mary Slessor and Ann Judson. Bad marks and good marks no doubt had their share in winning first place in that corporate competition. Eventually in my last year I was put in leadership positions: Prefect, head of Carmichael House and a Ranger Patrol leader.

Through the years we had occasional visits and holidays with our parents, but most of our young lives revolved around the school, where we were held to high academic standards. Our big goal was to complete Form Six and take the Oxford Matriculation examinations sent out from England. An Oxford certificate would give us entrance to most institutions of higher learning in the Western world. We had sports according to the season: field hockey, basketball swimming and rowing. My only sports achievement was in rowing, where because of my short size, I was often given the role of the cox steering.

We were given a thorough religious training on school days, including the twice-daily quiet times and short devotions in assembly known as Morning Prayers and Evening Prayers. On Sunday mornings we went to churches in the community.

A poignant memory was our two-mile crocodile march from the compound to Union Church each Sunday. As we walked through "Eau de Cologne Valley" as we called it, the stench of open Chinese sewers told us we were about half-way there.

During rest-time after lunch we were allowed to read only books "Passed for Sunday." These rules implanted in our minds a respect that Sunday was different and set apart for God. We had Sunday School in the afternoon and, before supper, we were required to write a home-letter, a habit which I have kept all my life. In the evening we had a meeting in the Memorial Hall in which all the students and staff on the compound met for a service of worship and a message often given by visiting speakers.

In spite of all the meetings we attended, the ones that made the greatest impact on me were the summer Children's Special Service Mission. (C.S.S.M.) meetings on the beach. Platforms and seating were dug out of the sand. Lanterns and decorations made the place festive. The singing was lively and messages were given by speakers gifted to share with young people. We had sand-building competitions in which we designed all sorts of creative texts or illustrations of a Biblical nature. It was at that beach, at the age of 14, that I was baptized one Sunday with fishermen mending their nets along the shore.

My most cherished memories are those connected with the Girl Guides and Rangers. Our Captain, Miss Phare, personally knew the founders, Lord and Lady Baden-Powell, in England. She and Miss MacNair inspired us with their talks and programs and the incentives to do all sorts of activities to earn badges. We had badges for Book Lovers, Gardeners, Friend to Animals and many others. There was much outlet for fun and creativity, for learning new things and for building character. With so much to do I never felt bored.

I did feel lonely sometimes when thinking of my Mother and Father. Separations from family were the hardest part of being an M.K. (missionary kid). We understood very early why we had to leave our parents. There were no suitable schools in the area where our parents worked, and as people called by God to preach the gospel in inland China, we knew they couldn't join us in Chefoo. We were blessed by dedicated and godly missionary-teachers who did their best to give us good care and supervision, but that didn't replace the regular love and care of parents.

One time when I was quite young, I decided I would not ever again be separated from my mother. I clung to her skirt at the train station and had to be wrenched from her to board the train. The fears of facing those awful partings, the heart-rending sobs and lonely longing became a repetitive hurdle to face and never got easier as we got older.

I remember the last goodbye when I was leaving China after graduation to take up further studies in Canada. The family decided to ease the strain by splitting the farewells into three sections; I gave my last hugs to my sisters in my Mother's office and waved goodbye to my Father at the hockey-field as I rode in a rickshaw to the ship accompanied by my Mother. I will never forget my Father's bent figure as he turned away collapsing in tears.

During three decades in China my parents endured long separations from their home countries, a devastating earthquake, bandits, political unrest, and countless other hardships, but they said to me years later that the separation from their own children was what cost them most.

What helped me and my sisters get through those times was a strong awareness that we were constantly loved, not abandoned. Little surprise presents were packed in our trunks for us to look forward to when we did our unpacking at school. Never an opportunity was missed to send us letters, messages, gifts and spending money so we felt well cared for. The candy cupboard was always stocked with sweets and goodies or jam to share with others. They demonstrated love in their absence in a manner which we as kids could interpret. We got the message clearly, "We love you!"

I don't recall that my parents ever quoted chapter and verse of Scripture to underscore the need for these long separations, but I believe the truths were written in our hearts. I now look back and see that God in His love had promised special benefits and comforts to those who make the sacrifices of separating from families, properties and careers to go out and serve Him. It is found in Luke 18:29-30. "I tell you the truth," Jesus said to them, "no one who has left home or wife or brothers or parents or children for the sake of the kingdom of God will fail to receive many times as much in this age and, in the age to come, eternal life."

Separation revealed to me a hidden truth of God's love. When we obey God out of love for Him, and separation from family is part of the cost, God multiplies love back to us. We may be separated from one another, but we are never separated from God's love. That love is often expressed through the hospitality of other homes and the kindnesses of friends and strangers who become our extended family. We may give up family, but we cannot out-give God.

In the test and triumph of a trial, we gain an authority as we prove God's faithfulness to those who trust Him. We grow in confidence to trust Him for greater things. We know the reality of His power to give us love and peace in the midst of difficult situations. I appreciate the privilege to feel compassion and to share God's love and peace with a fellow-sufferer. My years of separation were painful, but now we have the blessing of sharing our story as a way to comfort and calm troubled souls. This is a lasting gift of great joy — a treasure without price.

LEAVING CHINA — ALONE AND LOST

The closer our ship got to America, the more excited and anxious I became. I had often daydreamed about my future, but I truly didn't know what life would be like for me in this new land. War was breaking out in China as I was leaving Shanghai, and the world was filled with uncertainties. During our two-week voyage on board the SS President Coolidge I spent many hours on deck gazing at a world of water from horizon to horizon, broken only by waves and jumping fish and spectacular sunsets in the evenings.

En route we had made a one-day's stop in Honolulu, an island paradise that captivated me with its fragrant flowers, spectacular sights and happy Hawaiian music. World War II was raging in Europe and I had heard the bombs of the Sino-Japanese war as we left China. Hawaii seemed so safe and serene — the perfect place to be in a world at war. On that balmy day in August 1941, I could not have imagined that just four months later Japanese bombs would shatter that peaceful illusion by attacking the U.S. Navy fleet in Pearl Harbor. Nor could I have imagined that the SS President Coolidge would be sunk in the war that followed.

A few days later, our ship sailed through San Francisco's Golden Gate, the entry to a whole new life for me. Of the 25 of us traveling together in the missionary party, only two – Edvard Torjesen and myself — were without any family members. I was 17 years old, a fledgling out of a protected compound nest and as naive about the ways of the world as I could be. Thankfully, Mr. Griffin of the China Inland Mission Office, greeted us on arrival to help manage the red tape and sort out our travel arrangements. We were ordered to wait at the jetty while tickets, immigration papers, baggage details and various forms were completed. After hours of waiting, we were all herded to a restaurant for supper and then suddenly told to hurry to the train station across the street. Scrambling into the crowd, I noticed people carrying pink forms. I finally had to ask one of my companions:

"What are those pink papers?"

"They are train tickets."

"But, I don't have any," I shouted as we rushed along.

The voice called back to me, "Go back to the counter and there you will meet your friend Edvard and he will give it to you."

As I turned back, the station was a sea of faces, but not one I recognized anywhere. I dashed back to the train tracks just in time to watch a train slowly move out with no whistle or announcement. It quietly slipped away out of sight. It was dark. I was alone. Lost. I stood there in shock, staring at those empty tracks.

Did all my friends leave on that train? I worried. *Am I really here all by myself? What do I do next?* I had no address of anyone to contact in San Francisco or Los Angeles. I had no money. My purse was packed in my suitcase checked for Los Angeles. As an M.K. in school, we were always dependent on our escorts.

A porter noticed me and asked, "Do you need help, Ma'am?"

"I think all the people in my party have gone on the train and left me behind," I wailed. His help was to turn me over to a ticket agent who was just as bewildered about what to do with me as the porter. He referred me to the passenger agent. Each time I told my story the sadder it got and the more of a problem case I felt. Finally, a kind and trustworthy agent decided to send me across the city to another station. He suggested I attempt to rendezvous with some of our travel party headed for Philadelphia.

"But I don't want to leave you and I don't have any money to get a taxi," I cried. He assured me, "We'll take care of that and here is my card. Go and stand by a certain gate and everyone leaving on that train must pass through it. You'll meet the people you know that way."

It was my first ride in a Yellow cab. We sped across the city and I thought about the game of "Missing the train" which we played at school and found myself laughing at the absurdity of the reality. The next minute I felt scared not knowing where I would end up.

Arriving at the station I recognized a missionary couple. Hearing my story, they looked as perplexed as I felt. What were they to do with a lost teenager trying to connect to Canada when they were on their honeymoon to Philadelphia? Some helpful eavesdropper suggested the Travelers Aid. A lady at the wicket (counter) there looked down at me and said, "And what is your name, dear?" followed by, "And how old are you darlin'?" Here was the essence of sweet kindness and I relaxed until she took me into her office and phoned around the city.

"Yes!" she spoke with concern, "A girl of 17 lost in a strange city is a serious thing." Soon I began to wonder if my situation was more serious than I had thought. The phone rang again and I heard that Mr. Griffin, our escort from Los Angeles, was returning to pick me up.

What a happy reunion! We celebrated by going to a snack bar where I had my first milkshake. I was amazed at the huge metal container which kept refilling my regular-sized cup. I spent my first night at the YMCA and saw another New World "miracle" in the lobby. You put in a nickel and out of the machine came a red apple!

At last alone in my room that night I had time to reflect. I had no night clothes, no toothbrush, no Bible — and then I saw a Bible on the stand. Picking it up, I asked the Lord, *Why did this happen to me? I didn't want to be a trouble like this, but I have been nothing but trouble ever since I arrived!* At random I opened up to Philippians 4:6-7 and the words struck me. "Do not be anxious about anything, but in everything, by prayer and petition, with thanksgiving, present your requests to God."

It hit me hard. My first test of faith and I had failed. I had panicked and not prayed. The preceding verse says, "The Lord is near," but I had not been aware or even looked for Him. In that hotel room the Lord gave me a revelation of my need, both the diagnosis of anxiety and the prescription of prayer.

When I arrived at my destination in the China Inland Mission home in Toronto, Ontario, Canada, that very text was framed on the wall outside my room. I sensed that the Lord intended

me to get the message, "Do not be anxious. . .pray."
He underlined the importance by giving it to me
twice — on my arrival in the United States and
again on my arrival in Canada.

It is not enough to read the Bible and
memorize texts. I had been taught well by my
missionary parents and teachers and could quote
Scriptures. The prophet in Zechariah 13:9 quotes
the Lord,

"I will refine them like silver and test them
like gold.

They will call on my name and I will answer them. . ."

In refining tests, God's Word becomes real
to us. We no longer speak truths just through our
minds and lips. We have treasure, "more precious
than gold," as the Psalmist says, learned and stored
in our hearts and expressed through our lives
(Psalm 19:10).

PEACE AND PROVISION

When Japan launched its invasion of China, foreign missionaries clung to their neutral status for safety. Britain was not yet at war with Japan so British mission compounds like the one at Chefoo painted huge British flags on the roofs as a way to assure our protection. We could hear the bombs as Japanese planes attacked Chefoo, but we felt confident that the bombers would avoid us as they flew their deadly missions.

The Japanese attack on Pearl Harbor on December 7th, 1941, destroyed that safety net. Both the United States and Great Britain declared war against Japan, and with that declaration every British and American missionary in China was put at risk. Soon the Japanese army captured Chefoo and took over the Mission Compound, forcing all the residents (including my sisters) into internment camps. My parents were also captured and interned by the Japanese.

This was the beginning of three and a half years of silent separation from my family. Only twice during those years did I get any word from them, and then it was only a 10-word Red Cross message, assuring me that my parents and sisters were alive. Those brief messages took about a year to reach me via the Swiss Red Cross office, but I was unable to contact my family.

The separation from my earthly father meant that I leaned all the harder on my Heavenly Father. I prayed for wisdom in choosing a career and for comfort in my helplessness concerning my family. At that time I started doing prayer-walks from the Mission Home in Toronto to the Insurance Agency downtown where I worked as stenographer. The Lord led me to apply for nurse's training at the Toronto Western Hospital. At 5 feet, I was two inches below their minimum height, but they accepted me anyway! That was a sign to me that God had opened that door of opportunity for me. I joyfully resigned from my job as stenographer, excited over the prospects of wearing a nurse's uniform and learning to care for the sick.

The Scripture which came to me as I started on this new career puzzled me. "Beloved, think it not strange concerning the fiery trial which is to try you, as though some strange thing happened unto you: But rejoice, inasmuch as you are partakers of Christ's sufferings; that, when his glory shall be revealed, you may be glad also with exceeding joy" (Peter 4:12-13, KJV). Hardly an encouragement to launch out on a new career.

One day Mr. Brownlee, the Mission Home Director who was acting as guardian for me, gave me some serious news. "Ottawa has frozen all accounts of internees so I have no more access to your father's account." Having power of attorney, Mr. Brownlee had been giving me about $5 a month, enough for a few stamps, street-car fares and the treat of a few pieces of fruit.

Now my only income had dried up. I will forever be grateful that he had the courage not to bail me out of my problem, but wisely instructed me to go back to the residence and get on my knees and pray to my Heavenly Father. For a brief time on the streetcar, I indulged in a pity party, *Poor me, no money, my family all in concentration camp in China. . .I did pray after all about going into nurses' training.* Another voice inside spoke up, *Stop it! Pray!*

I knelt by my bed at the nurses' residence and prayed, "Dear Lord, You have always provided for the missionaries and us M.K.'s — we've been well fed, well clothed, well educated and all our needs have been met through all my life. Now Lord, I asked You about coming into training and I believe You led me here. What do you want me to do? Do You want me to stop training and go out and get a job? Is it possible You want to provide for me now like you cared for the missionaries? I am willing to do whatever You want me to do."

When I got up from my knees I was strangely aware of a gift of peace, the peace that was beyond my understanding. I was no longer anxious about finances or the decision to continue my nursing training. This special peace stayed with me during my years in school and was observed by colleagues who asked, "How can you be at peace with all your family in danger so far away?" It was God's gift.

A few days after that prayer I got a call from an Anglican priest who said he wanted to see me. I thought perhaps I'd said something to one of his parishioners in the hospital that didn't jibe with his theology. I half expected a scolding when I got to his office, but instead he greeted me warmly. Then to my even greater surprise he said, "I have a patient who recently underwent surgery and promised the Lord that she would give Him a thank offering when He brought her through. The first person she thought of coming out of anaesthesia was you, her nurse. She knew it was not ethical for you to receive money from a patient, but I am giving it to you as a gift from the Lord."

As I walked back to the residence with three months' spending money in my hand, the thought struck me, *God is my Heavenly Father. He has heard my prayer. He is providing for me as He provided for the missionaries!* I felt praise to God come out of the depths of my being until I caught myself exclaiming, "Hallelujah! Hallelujah!" Thinking that other pedestrians would wonder if I was crazy, I clapped my hand on my mouth to stop erupting in loud bursts of joyful thanks.

In the following weeks and months, many surprises came through the mail. Not only were gifts of money enclosed in letters and cards, but when some donors received my notes of thanks, they promptly surprised me again by duplicate gifts.

One day a bad snow storm came to Toronto and all milk deliveries and mail deliveries were held up. Only one special delivery letter came to me at the residence all the way from Australia. It was a gift of money from relatives of my father who had been hostile to his missionary service and who had no idea of my state of need. I marveled at this provision from afar. It was a sermon in the snow. Not even the elements could hold back a loving Father's care for a trusting child!

One time a China missionary was speaking at a church in Maryland, and he had made in passing a reference about a nursing trainee in Toronto whose missionary parents were interned in China. Without naming me he cited God's provision for me though I had not solicited funds (which was against the policy of the China Inland Mission). Afterward, a couple approached the speaker and explained that God had told them to donate anonymously to this student nurse for the rest of her training! They neither knew me nor my parents — it was truly a love-gift through them from the Lord.

I ended up three times richer trusting my Heavenly Father than when I was dependent on my earthly father. God's Word had instructed me not to be anxious, but to pray with thanksgiving, and I would have peace that passes understanding. In Philippians 4:19, it says, "My God will meet all your needs." When we do not have much in our own purse, I discovered that our Heavenly Father has all that we need in His.

ONE HEART AND ONE WAY

I first set eyes on the love of my life as I lay in my hospital bed, recovering from the ravages of encephalitis, a serious virus infection of the brain. The disease was endemic in the Toronto area, and I became ill just three months before my graduation from the School of Nursing at Toronto Western Hospital. I was hospitalized for two months, and during that time a girlfriend visited me and brought along her boyfriend, Douglas Feaver. He looked quite striking in his Canadian Air Force uniform. In chatting I discovered that Douglas had spent four years training pilots in flying and navigation during World War II. I learned much more about this young officer when I shared an apartment with his girlfriend. I had to endure a year of convalescence before I was well enough to complete my nurses' training, and during those months my friend would often effervesce about her romance as she read to me from Douglas' love letters.

We next met on the University of Toronto campus where Douglas headed up the Victoria College InterVarsity Christian Fellowship chapter, and I led the group from the graduate School of Nursing. We and others representing separate Colleges called ourselves "The Cabinet," and we met regularly to strategize and pray over our corporate evangelical witness on the campus.

Douglas caught my attention as a unique character, unconventional and interesting. One time he suddenly broke out in French and then apologized, explaining that he had just been absorbed in reading French! He might burst into the room with his over-sized cello or relax by putting his feet on the table so we all observed the holes in his shoes. His bright mind exploded with vision and caught our imagination. I saw him as the real dynamic center of the group, leading with ideas. After his romance with my roommate had broken up, I wondered if he was a potential date for me. But he never seemed to notice me so my interest quickly waned.

About a year later we found ourselves serving at the Pioneer Boys Camp in Ontario. Douglas was Music Director and I was camp nurse. There were about 200 boys in this Christian camp, well known for its standards in camping skills and character building. The intense six-week program took its toll on the counselors. By the last two weeks, more leaders than campers came to the Infirmary seeking help for infections or medical problems and Douglas joined the parade. It happened to be a two-week period when there was no resident doctor in the camp so I was left in charge to treat the patients.

I started by ordering hot compresses for the boil on his arm which I treated every few hours, giving us time to enjoy long conversations. As this went on, the boil got worse (I suspect from over-treatment). Next I decided to lance and drain the boil. But when I saw the amount of infection, I also ordered Douglas to the infirmary for rest and antibiotic shots. Penicillin was a relatively new drug, and I tremble today at the risk I took with

Douglas given the allergic reactions which many have suffered. Thankfully, he did recover, and I like to say that I hooked him at the end of a hypodermic needle! After that incident, we looked at each other with new eyes and knew our hearts were warming up!

When camp ended we had only had a few days together before Douglas had to return to Baltimore to finish his graduate studies at Johns Hopkins University . He called me right away for a date and so began what we like to call our two-week whirlwind courtship. As we grew closer during those days, we felt God had truly custom-made our past history, personalities and dreams to fit one another. Our friends and families were fully supportive and as we prayed together each evening, we sensed that we had God's blessing too. With marriage now on the horizon, Douglas decided to seal our commitment by sharing his final secret and joy.

"Margaret," he announced, "I am a missionary candidate for China. My application papers are with the China Inland Mission right now."

Douglas thought sure this announcement would bring me great delight. He was stunned when he saw the look of shock on my face.

"I have already been turned down by that Mission for medical reasons," I said with a shaky voice. The impact of that sober moment hit us hard. We knew we had an immediate choice to make: my will, our will, or God's?

We knew we did not dare to live apart from God, losing the blessing of obeying and serving Him. The choice was made. I must free Douglas to go where the Lord led him and not stand in his way. Painfully we decided to sever our relationship. No more dates, letters, or phone calls. It had to be radical and sincere. We agreed that our lives belonged to God, and He was the only One who could say our lives belonged to each other.

I remember getting down on my knees beside my bed, wracked in anguished prayer. My whole being sobbed. I cried out for help to release the man I loved to God though my heart still clung to him. It was a prayer often repeated during those heartrending days.

A few weeks later I received an unexpected call from Douglas in Baltimore, Maryland. He had just received a letter from the China Inland Mission headquarters in Philadelphia telling him that they could *not* accept his application because the Mission had decided to bring all its missionaries out of China in light of dangers posed by the new Communist regime. In closing, the Mission leaders made one final observation: "Looking over your application and recommendations, we feel that you should be a missionary to the academic world. We suggest that you continue to pursue your Ph.D. at this time."

We had no hesitation in recognizing God giving us back to each other. There is a promise given to Israel in Jeremiah 32:39 which reads, "I will give them one heart, and one way, that they may fear me for ever, for the good of them, and of their children after them" (KJV).

We had been given one heart and God confirmed His gift of us to each other by giving us one way. This verse became our marriage motto, a spiritual gift we have given to many others. A costly sacrifice made to God is never wasted. His blessing upon it makes the gift worth infinitely more.

JOYS OF GIVING

Our first year of marriage, 1950, was the final year of graduate study before Douglas earned his Ph.D. at Johns Hopkins University in Baltimore, Maryland. We were as happy as lovebirds as we "nested" in a bright Chinese-pink apartment. The best thing about our little place was that it was within easy walking distance of the University and Memorial Hospital, where I worked as a Clinical Instructor.

One day I cut my hand on a tin can and the hospital authorities decided to give me a tetanus antitoxin shot. Within five days my glands began to swell up from an allergic reaction to the shot. Hives covered my body and my face swelled until my eyes became slits. Hospital staff tried every treatment they could, but I knew I was sinking fast. I began to lose consciousness, and when I saw my blue finger nails, I realized I might be dying.

Two thoughts flashed into my mind: *I am prepared to die.* I felt no fear because I knew where I was going to spend eternity. The second thought was a regret: *I will meet the Lord with so little to show Him for my time on earth.* I wished I had loved Him more, followed Him more closely, given to Him more generously, and served Him more faithfully.

As I went into cardiac collapse, six nurses and three doctors rushed to my side to attend me.

The senior resident intern reached for a vial of a new drug, cortisone, which he had kept in his room for just such an emergency. With no time to spare, not even time to call Douglas to the hospital to sign permission, he administered this new drug. Slowly my vital signs improved. My life was spared.

The next day as soon as Douglas arrived at the hospital to visit me, he was quickly ushered into the office. There they urged him to sign papers releasing the hospital authorities from all responsibility or lawsuits relating to the administration of the new drug. When he heard how the cortisone had saved my life, he signed the papers with gratitude.

In the following days a parade of doctors from Johns Hopkins Hospital and School of Medicine came to see this phenomenon of recovery from anaphylactic shock from a tetanus antitoxin shot. I felt like Exhibit A as the medical staff and students discussed my case around my bed.

After my recovery, a medical doctor friend and his wife in Canada surprised us by sending a gift of $100 to help with the hospital expenses. Today, this would be comparable to a gift of $1,000. We were deeply touched by their kindness, but did not feel we really needed the help just then. Their thoughtful gesture of love brought its own gift of healing.

A short time later we were invited to a secret meeting where we heard a visiting pastor from East Germany sharing about the hardships of his people in the post-war situation. He told about orphans and limited resources to care for the children. We had so much and these were in need of food and clothing. Douglas and I quickly agreed that we should be generous and give half of our gift from Canada to this pastor, which we did. However, when we came home we felt neither peace nor joy over our donation. What was wrong? We talked it over and received an impression. It was like an inner voice speaking to our hearts, *Give it all to the Lord. Don't keep any of it for yourselves.* We both agreed we were to pass on the full $100 we had been given by our friends. We knew this was right. We gave and our hearts were at peace again.

Some time later we received a wonderful acknowledgment of our gift. We were informed that the money provided shoes for 22 orphans. God healed me, giving me another chance to live and walk with Him on earth. He also gave us the unique opportunity to help His little ones so they could walk with shoes on their feet. As Jesus said, "It is more blessed to give than to receive (Acts 20:35)." The joy He put in our hearts put a spring in our steps.

BROKEN HEARTS

Toward the end of our first year of marriage Douglas and I were thrilled to discover we were expecting a child. A few weeks later our joy turned into anxiety as hemorrhaging threatened to take this precious life. I was ordered to stay in bed and move as little as possible. For a week we waited in desperate hope. Sadly, my heart pains kept rhythm with the labor contractions which inevitably expelled the embryo.

This happened in the middle of the night and Douglas went out on the streets in a wild search for a telephone to call a taxi. The doctors did an emergency surgery at four o'clock in the morning. I felt weak from the loss of blood and the loss of a child. As a professional nurse I had never realized the grief of a miscarriage. In fact, the official record described it as a "spontaneous abortion" — a term which horrified my husband when he saw it. I reflected on the many patients in hospital who had undergone similar surgery to mine. *I gave them good nursing care but I never imagined the emotional pain they were suffering. I now can understand. Like me, they were feeling grief.*

Douglas was under double stress. The week before his final exams he was trying to care for me while I was confined in bed. The week ended early Sunday morning with him rushing his hemorrhaging wife to the hospital. On Sunday

TITHING ON A TIGHT BUDGET

Douglas graduated from Johns Hopkins University with a Ph.D. in classical studies, and we wondered what we were to do and where we were to go. His professors urged Douglas to apply for a Fellowship grant to do post-doctoral study in Athens at the American School of Classical Studies. This award would be won by a national competition and, since we were past the deadline for entry with a written sample of one's work, we dismissed the challenge. The persuasion and pressure of the professors won out however and, reluctantly, Douglas applied. To our surprise, he was awarded the Fellowship and we concluded that God intended for us to go to Greece.

The next surprise in this adventure of faith was learning that I was pregnant. The happy news, coming just a few weeks before our departure, was tempered by an acute morning sickness condition called *hyperemesis gravidarum*. I felt violently nauseated much of the day, certainly not the way I wanted to start our trans-Atlantic voyage on board the Italian ship, *Italia*.

When it seemed that I couldn't possibly feel worse, our ship was hit by a hurricane and began to roll. The waves rose 60 feet and the ship shuddered on the crests of the enormous waves and seemed to sink in the depths of watery valleys. Waves splashed on the decks and the iron doors were locked to keep our cabins dry. In the dining room the waiters swayed and the dishes flew. I felt so turbulent within that surviving the turbulence at sea did not frighten me. I felt too weak to fight, the fury of the storm too strong. I looked at our life jackets hanging up in the cabin closet, waiting for the emergency warning. We ignored them. We knew that we would have no chance to survive the ferocity of the storm if the ship did not hold. Douglas sat beside me, feeling quite helpless.

Stirred by compassion, he softly began to sing a hymn:

O the deep, deep love of Jesus, Vast, unmeasured, boundless, free:

Rolling as a mighty ocean In its fulness over me.

Underneath me, all around me, Is the current of Thy love;

Leading onward, leading homeward, To my glorious rest above.

His tender caring, and the comfort of those words, calmed the storm within me.

Outside the storm continued and we had to change course to get out of the worst of it. When we arrived at the school in Athens, we again found ourselves under the weather — this time, financially. I had anticipated working as a nurse, but found out that, as a Canadian, there were no jobs available to me. The cost of living at the American School was $180 per month; $60 for our one room, $60 each for food. Our financial stipend came to $200 a month. That left us $20 to spare which also represented the tithe of our income. It appeared that we had the choice of robbing God of the percentage we owed to Him or going into debt. We had a lifetime commitment to the biblical teaching of giving tithes and offerings. We might sink financially, but we wanted to honor the Lord and make the choice to give to Him and not to ourselves.

We visited our Greek pastor, George Hadjiantoniou, and explained our situation, "This is a special sacrifice for us and we wonder if there is a special need in the congregation which our gift could meet?" Indeed, there was a widow whose only means of support was through her son. He had been called to join the army, but would receive so little that it would be insufficient to feed the mother.

"You will be surprised," he said, "but your gift will be adequate to feed her, given her style of living." We were thankful for the privilege of helping this needy widow.

The American School had made a new rule and we were the first test case. No children, not even newborns, were permitted in residence. The postwar living was difficult: we had running water for three hours every other day; the food was poor and outside housing was out of the question. Painfully, we concluded that I would have to return to Canada early, leaving Douglas to complete the academic year. This was a heart-wrenching decision and was made more stressful by the sudden awareness that we would end up $1,000 in debt. Being debt-free was a fundamental value to us and I began to panic. How had we gone wrong?

Desperate, I knelt in prayer and poured out my heart of anxiety to the Lord. "Oh Lord, are we out of your will being here in Greece? We prayed for guidance and didn't you lead us here? I am ashamed to be so deeply in debt. Yet, Lord, it says in your Book that the cattle on a thousand hills are Yours [Psalm 50:10]. You have all resources to meet all needs. Please forgive us where we are wrong and please have mercy and rescue us." God answers heart cries and I knew He heard mine.

The ordeal of parting from each other came all too soon. Being seven months pregnant, we had to get special permission for me to fly to Rome and then London. It was mid-winter and the Cunard Lines also granted special permission for me to board the Queen Mary for the ocean voyage to New York. From there I traveled by train to Toronto where I lived with my family during the six months of our separation.

A few days after my return the telephone rang. "This is to inform you that one of Douglas's great-Aunts has decided to give out some of her gold mine wealth to all her relatives. You are to receive $1,000." In that moment I recognized the answer to my prayer from the One who owns the cattle on a thousand hills.

Meanwhile, Douglas completed his post-doctoral graduate year at the American School of Classical Studies in Athens, Greece. It was a good year during which he researched the excavations and mapped out the city of Corinth as it would have looked at the time of St. Paul.

Douglas waited several weeks for the news that he was a father. Was it a girl or a boy? The wait was excruciating. Then one day he received word that a courier would be arriving with a telegram in a few hours. With excitement he raced up Acro-Corinth, and set a school record for climbing that peak. The courier came with good news: David Stephen Feaver had safely arrived. Three months later Douglas would meet his son in the train station at Toronto and hold him in his arms for the first time.

When it came time for Douglas to leave Greece, he looked forward to an exciting reunion, but first he wanted to know how the widow in the Church would manage.

"Oh," the pastor said, "You will hardly believe this. Her son has just received a promotion. It is big enough for him to carry on with her support."

God cares for the widow and He cares for the poor. We also discovered He is faithful and loving to us when we cry out to Him in crises. We cannot out-give God. He is no one's debtor. We placed our little treasure in His hand and He paid our debts with dividends of joy.

A PILGRIMAGE TO THE STABLE

In 1951 Douglas and I left Athens, Greece, where he was doing post-doctoral studies in archaeology, for a trip to the Holy Land. A Lutheran professor, Matthew Wiencke, also a research student at the American School of Classical Studies in Athens, joined us on this journey. We flew from Athens to Cyprus and made a short stopover in Beirut, Lebanon. We drove by taxi to Damascus through snow drifts so high that it took hours of waiting to move in the one lane of traffic.

As we wandered around the city of Damascus I was fascinated by a woman walking with dignity and poise with a basket of live chickens balanced on her head. "Matt, you must take a picture of that!" I ordered. Matt felt some reluctance but he succumbed to my persuasion and pleasure.

We entered the mosque for a tour and were given gestures to sit down and take off our shoes and put on the paper slippers provided. I was quietly marveling that I, as a foreign woman, would be permitted to visit the interior of a mosque. A small delegation of men came to the door and engaged our guide in animated conversation. He came back to us and indicated we were to put our shoes on and follow him outside.

We found ourselves escorted by a couple of men down the street called Straight not knowing where we were being led. *I feel uneasy about this. Where are we going? Something is wrong.* As I looked up I noticed a building with barred windows and I said to Douglas, "You know, I think we are under arrest." Sure enough, we were ushered into a police department and asked about the photograph we had taken of a peasant woman without permission. Firmly they demanded that we give up the camera. Both Douglas and Matt were ready to comply in their eagerness to avoid causing further offense.

But I was offended at the loss of our pictures and camera which had been borrowed for this tour. I boldly defended our actions which we had not understood were illegal. Douglas and Matt tried to calm me down and the police officers appeared agitated at alarming a very pregnant foreigner. They told us to come back at the end of the day and we would be able to retrieve the camera, but not the pictures, which have been indelibly photographed in my mind!

After this adventure we left Damascus by taxi for a memorable Christmas Eve journey to Jerusalem. At one point on this day-long drive we were all told to get out of the car on the side of the road. *Do we have car problems? Is there some danger?* We watched a caravan of vehicles coming and realized we had moved to clear the way for the King of Jordan to pass by. We felt a sense of significance. We were part of a pilgrimage of people from around the world on their way to Bethlehem this Christmas Eve to celebrate the first coming of our King Jesus.

As we drove on in the dark hours we listened to the beautiful carol, "I wondered as I wandered out under the sky how Jesus, our Savior, did come for to die." We looked up to the bright stars shining on this clear night and wondered if the Wise Men also had traveled along this ancient trail. Our souls were lifted to heaven in worship as we listened to parts of Handel's "Messiah" from Radio Jerusalem. We would never forget this night.

Suddenly a strange sound assaulted our ears. Weird Arabic music came over the radio and our trance was broken in a moment of revelation. "Margaret," said my husband in a painful tone, "I've just realized something. Probably the angels sounded more like *this* local music than the 'Messiah!'"

We arrived in Jerusalem in the evening and got another taxi to take us to Bethlehem. There was still time to get to the Church of the Nativity before midnight. Because of the political tensions between the Arabs and Israel, we could not travel the five-mile route to Bethlehem. We had to drive 40 miles through the Valley of Gehenna around hairpin turns on precipitous mountain roads. *Our driver and the Arab chauffeurs we see drive their taxis at reckless speeds. What are we doing endangering our lives like this?* It was not unwarranted fear. That night, as taxis were racing between Jerusalem and Bethlehem, at least one car hurtled down the mountain killing a French professor.

It was a moving experience to join pilgrims from many nations coming together to celebrate Christ's birth. We praised the Lord singing carols in the courtyard of the Church of the Nativity. There we glimpsed the place where Jesus is believed to have been born. Bells chimed which were broadcast around the world. We had a profound sense of joyous history.

On Christmas day we attended the Anglican Cathedral and experienced another blissful moment. As the Scripture in the first chapter of Luke was read, we listened to the words: "And Mary arose in those days, and went into the hill country with haste, into a city of Judah; And entered into the house of Zacharias, and saluted Elisabeth. And it came to pass, that, when Elisabeth heard the salutation of Mary, the babe leaped in her womb. . ." (Luke 1:39-41, KJV). At that precise moment the babe in my own womb "leaped" and I spontaneously jumped up from my seat!

Years later we found ourselves celebrating Christmas in Bethlehem, Pennsylvania, with our four children and many Christian friends. The Bethlehem Christian Fellowship group met in our large home, and we traditionally celebrated by providing gifts and a party for the girls in the Lehigh County Jail. We also took gifts of turkeys and goodies to some of our needy friends. As usual we decorated our home, trying to transform it into a palace to celebrate the first coming of the King.

This particular year our hearts were heavy. Conflict had come into the family and one couple felt their marital tension so deeply that they separated for the holidays. I felt the shadow of sorrow and shame creeping over my soul and I could not bear the burden of this guilt.

I remember driving to deliver some of our gifts to the poor and feeling no joy in the giving because of the grief we were giving as a family to the Lord.

I poured out my pain to Him, "All our preparations are in vain. We have tried to make our home beautiful for You, but we are acting like animals. Our home is as dirty and messy as a stable." I'll never forget His voice of comfort speaking into the silence inside me, "I came to a stable the first time and I'm willing to come again."

Oh! Thank you, Lord Jesus.

FRUITFUL FAILURES

After Douglas returned from Greece, we moved to New Haven, Connecticut, to start our life as a family of three. Douglas was given a four-year position as lecturer at Yale University. We often joked that half of his salary was paid in prestige. We could not afford rental housing in New Haven on the annual income of $3,500. We moved eight miles from the campus to find lower rental accommodations in East Haven. There we lived among a community of students and faculty, occupying winterized cottages by the ocean.

As a Christian I wanted to share my faith with my neighbors and invited them to come to a fellowship Bible study group held weekly in my home. Only two accepted the invitation, both of them wives of husbands attending the Episcopal Seminary. Their husbands would commute with Douglas each day, a drive which often ended up in heated debates over doctrines and religious issues.

I took the little Bible Study seriously, spending hours in careful study and preparation. Before many weeks had passed, Jane chose to drop out, clearly uncomfortable with my simple, evangelical approach. Perhaps I represented what her husband was choosing to leave behind. He had come from a legalistic, fundamentalist background and was embracing more and more of the formality and practices of the high Episcopal Church. He eventually graduated, became a Roman Catholic, and finally became secretary to a well-known New York Cardinal.

I carried on the study, but it wasn't long before Mary left too, for reasons that saddened me. Before coming to Yale, her husband Keith had made a fortune in the Texas oil business, but he had become bored with his work and the lifestyle of the wealthy. In time he decided he wanted to do something for God and chose to train for the clergy. But at seminary he didn't see the reality he was looking for and, disillusioned by all the hypocrisy, dropped out of school to return to the oil business.

I had to face it — my first neighborhood outreach ministry was a complete failure.

Ten years later we were attending a fellowship group in the home of a friend who personally knew Mary. This hostess decided to put us back in contact with her, and shortly afterwards we received an unforgettable letter. Keith wrote how he had gone back into the Texas oil business, but still felt lonely, lost, confused, unfulfilled.

He went on to describe how one day while walking alone in the woods, he heard God speak to him, "Keith, all I ever wanted from you is your heart, not your works. I just want you as you are." He was stunned by a revelation of God's love — an unconditional love willing to accept him and bless him without his earning it. He met Jesus and committed his whole life to Him there, stripped of all his previous goals and achievements.

A few months later, on their way to New York, Keith and Mary visited us in our home in Bethlehem, Pennsylvania. We marveled at our "new" friends. They were both in love with Jesus. Keith was no longer searching in his confusion, but confident in his new peace. We felt our own hearts lit by the glow of joy emanating from their faith in their new Friend. Keith Miller wrote his story in the best seller, *The Taste of New Wine.*

In Psalm 126:5 we read that those who weep, carrying precious seed with them, shall return with songs of joy. We could not trace the spiritual growth to any specific seed of truth we had sown. Yet we experienced harvest-joy in our hearts. After a silence of ten years God brought a neighbor back to us, with a gift of encouragement hidden in his story for us. This couple's story was much like one Jesus told in a parable. The kingdom of God is like someone who found treasure in a field. Excited, they sold everything to buy that field (Matthew 13:44.) It may not have been our ministry, but our neighbor had bought the message we carried: Jesus loves you and, if you seek Him, you will find He is your treasure.

HOUSING HASSLES

Living on the meager salary of a Yale lecturer made it difficult to find adequate, convenient housing. We considered ourselves blessed to find the little cottage on the Atlantic Ocean in East Haven, Connecticut. Other young faculty and students lived near us in similar vacation cottages, which rented for a quarter of the price they cost during the summer season.

Living near the sea was a joy for us until a hurricane thundered in and wrecked our little community. We watched helplessly as the water slowly rose until it covered our car. Our Italian neighbors across the street were getting into a little boat and inwardly, I mocked them for leaving. Surely the worst was past. But the water continued to rise and soon we saw refrigerators and other big equipment swept along in the current. I found myself calling out, "Come and rescue us, too!"

As our little son got into the boat, he sighed, "Oh dear! Oh dear!" My own sigh was within. I had been caught mocking, just like the neighbors in Noah's day. I forgot that love and respect are essential elements in reaching out to neighbors. This time I almost missed the boat!

That flood motivated us to move the next year to a third-floor apartment above the Manse of our Church in New Haven. No flood was likely to reach us up there. Unfortunately, we didn't get to stay long in our safe little nesting place. The teaching assignment at Yale came to an end and we faced another move. Douglas accepted a teaching position at Lehigh University in Bethlehem, Pennsylvania, so once again we had to go apartment hunting. Kind friends took care of our two boys, four-year-old David and two-year-old John, to free us to drive down to Bethlehem for the day. After advertising in the local paper ahead of time, we prayed, "Dear Lord, could You find us an apartment on a second floor level? It is so tiring carrying babies and paraphernalia up three flights of stairs." There were no doubts about God's ability to answer that prayer, or that He would. He knew our needs and the one-day limit for apartment-hunting.

After arriving in Bethlehem, it came as a shock to discover not one suitable place for rent. Either the rent was too high or the space inadequate. *I know this is not God's provision for us.* Purchasing a home was not an option on our tight budget. Our hearts were confused. *Had the Lord forgotten there was only one day to settle this matter?* The day had to be spent somehow. Against our better judgment and feeling it was a futile exercise, we set out to look at houses for sale. We knew with our limited resources we were out of the market for purchasing housing. Therefore, dreaming about owning our own home never entered our minds.

During the last hour of our day we stopped to look at a small ranch-style home. It was owned by the Lehigh R.O.T.C. instructor and his wife who were leaving for California. It was a neat little home built the year before with tall poplar trees by the driveway and a cherry tree in front. Other fruit trees were planted in the back yard which would make a nice play area for children.

The moment of truth arrived and an incredible offer was made, "There have been other interested parties, but you seem to be the ones who would fit most happily into this nice neighborhood. With another home in California there is no need for us to make a profit on this deal. We are willing to sell the house for the balance owing and take responsibility for the mortgage. This way you can avoid fussing over a bank loan. Just carry on the same monthly mortgage payments and mail them to us. Due to special privileges with our R.O.T.C. status, the down payment will be only $600." We did have $600 in the bank although that would empty our account.

Is this really You, God? We only asked to rent a second floor apartment. Are you saying we can buy our own home? In a few minutes it was time to leave for dinner with the Classics Professor. He could not believe our story and decided to investigate the situation, check over the house, and convince himself that this was an honest deal. After his examination of both the house and the owners, he was assured that it was a bargain indeed. That sealed the decision in our hearts. The offer was accepted. The sudden decision almost stunned us with excitement and disbelief.

Arrangements were made to stay overnight and see a lawyer in the morning to sign papers. It was a sleepless night for me. In faith we had prayed for God to meet our need according to our understanding, but God was giving us so much more. . .our own home. It felt too good to be true.

On moving day, the four of us set out on our eight-hour road trip from New Haven to Bethlehem towing a U-Haul trailer jammed full of all our worldly possessions. The backseat of the car was packed full too so the boys had to sit up front with us. I was six months pregnant at the time, exhausted from packing, sweltering from 100-degree heat outside, and increasingly irritated by sharing a seat with two wiggly boys.

We must have looked like tired tramps as we arrived in Bethlehem. And as we unpacked our assortment of second-hand furniture, our neighbors no doubt wondered what had landed in their comfortable community. Our charming new home began to look like a dumping ground and with no curtains on the windows all our curious neighbors could easily peer in. I began to feel ashamed at our bare barn decor and immediately started shopping in my mind. I made mental lists of missing items and rearranged the order of priorities of need. *A dining table or a vacuum cleaner? Curtains or a garbage pail?*

My frustration was compounded by the fact that in this transition from Yale to Lehigh we would be two months without any income. As much as I wanted to spruce up our new home, I had to resign myself to the fact that it would be enough of a challenge just to keep our family fed. During those two months I had lots of time to plan my purchases, but without any means to shop, I began to feel increasingly obsessed and irritated. *Why am I so materially preoccupied? I thought things were not that important to me. I must get my thoughts on a different track. All the joy of this new home has gone out of the window. . .a picture window without curtains makes me feel like we're living in a glass house.*

I tried to pray but I had no peace. I knew I had to get my priorities straight, but how? When my husband arrived home from a doctor's visit with a preoperative slip in his hand, suddenly the curtains were forgotten. The surgery would be scheduled about the time our third child was due to arrive. (This would force Douglas to convalesce for six weeks, during the busy and difficult time of handling the new baby.) The jolt of this news brought both of us to an acute awareness of our desperate need of God's help. We fell on our knees beside each other and wept, *"Oh God, help us and show us where we have gone wrong. We are confused and we've lost our peace and joy. We feel lost. Help us, show us the way."*

The first miracle took place as soon as we got up on our feet. I looked at those windows and for the first time in weeks, they did not bother me. God gave a new perspective and a different point of view. The second miracle was a gift of healing. Douglas never needed the surgery, and we still have that preoperative slip in our family archives. A third surprise came as a stranger knocked on our door and introduced himself as one from the community coming to welcome us to the area. He said we had mutual friends in Connecticut, contractors who had recently moved to a bigger home. He went on to explain, "These friends say they have some golden drapes which they no longer need and they wondered if you would be interested in having them?" Golden drapes to enhance our yellow-painted house! For ten years those beautiful drapes adorned our windows.

From this experience we learned the power of praying as a team of two, both husband and wife, together. Jesus promised He would be present in a special way where two or three meet together, seeking Him (Matthew 18:19). He hears our heart cries, and He heard ours. He has the power to provide a home or a mere item to make that home attractive. He has the power to heal physically and emotionally in an instant of time.

He handed us a key to open the treasury of His good blessings which He was waiting to give to us. Praying not alone, but as one, together. Praying with broken hearts, open to God and each other. He meets us there.

EXPERIMENTS IN PRAYER

One of the highlights of our lives after we moved to Bethlehem in 1956 was our weekly fellowship meetings with other young parents from First Presbyterian Church. There were about a dozen of us, and most of the group were new at Bible study and corporate prayer. We found them to be hungry spiritually, and we saw familiar Scriptures with the fresh wonder as they came alive in their hearts.

When Douglas and I shared our testimonies of answered prayer we could see some of them listening wistfully. *Oh Lord, You hear all your children who call out to You. How can they learn that You have no favorites and we are not unique in having our prayers answered? Lord, help them grow in faith.*

Minutes later Paul casually brought up a prayer request which we would take with us to pray about. The more he detailed the problems the more I felt this was a major opportunity for all of us. His friend in Washington, DC was struggling with depression and anxiety. His wife was expecting another baby. His company was moving him to Tennessee. He had financial concerns having to sell his house in Washington and not able to afford mortgage and rent costs at the same time. But he needed a place to live in Tennessee.

In a burst of faith I challenged the group, "I believe that if we all agree to pray every day for a month for this man and his family, God will show us His answer by the time the month is up. Let's make a commitment to pray earnestly and see what God will do." The group took the challenge but I went home with a second thought, *What have we done? Is this faith or folly?*

It was two weeks later, halfway through our month's prayer experiment. Douglas was playing the cello and I was accompanying him on the piano when the phone rang. It was Paul with the latest news, "The friend we are praying for found a place to live with an elderly relative. But his house in Washington hasn't sold and worse yet, the lady in the house he was living in fell down the stairs and fractured her hip."

In a desperate attempt to encourage faith and prayer to continue in this additional tragedy, I found myself saying to him, "Well, we are not going to give up. There is a saying, 'Man's extremity is God's opportunity' so let's keep believing for a miracle." I went back to the piano deep in thought, *What a hypocrite I am. Those words were platitudes. I'm as distressed as Paul is. Is this experiment going to fail?*

The piano bench became an altar of intense intercession. Douglas and I cried our hearts out to the Lord, *"Oh Lord, forgive us if we have been presumptuous. We know we are not to tempt and test the Lord, but we longed for our friends to see Your power at work and to know that You will answer their prayers as You have ours. Lord, if we have been wrong and displeased You in what we have done and said, please forgive us and redeem our mistakes."*

A few days later Paul burst into our house and began to pace up and down in our living room saying, "It's a miracle! I can't believe it! I can't believe it!"

"Paul, what's happened?" I asked. "The company has done an unprecedented thing. They have reversed their plan and sent my friend back to Washington. He's back in his own home with his family. The house doesn't have to be sold. And his health is already improving. Just like that! Our prayers have been answered." *Thank You Lord for redeeming our mistakes and answering these prayers!*

Some years later our new Pastor, Lloyd Ogilvie, who later became chaplain to the U.S. Senate, decided to initiate fellowship groups throughout the membership. These were called Koinonia groups and Douglas and I were two of 40 chosen to launch this fellowship experiment. When we saw the names of about 16 who had signed up to join our group we were baffled. We not only did not know the church members but they represented the prominent, well-to-do leaders in the professional and business community. We felt intimidated and decided to let them face the culture shock of our contrasting lifestyles at our first meeting. We knew they lived in mansions but we initiated our group by inviting them to our small ranch-style home. We sat shoulder to shoulder in our hot and stuffy house with beads of perspiration dropping down our cheeks. Yet to our surprise, these church members were enthusiastic though, after that first time, we circulated among their beautiful air-conditioned homes.

When it came time to pray Douglas suggested, "I will start and, when as many of you wish to have prayed, Margaret will close." Douglas started. Pause. Margaret closed. *Oh Lord, these dear people have been church members much longer than we have, but they're not used to praying out loud. What shall we do? We need to break the sound barrier of prayer.*

At the next meeting we reminded the group that we teach even our two-year-olds to say "Thank you." We suggested that God would like to hear just a sentence prayer beginning with the words, "Thank you." Not a paragraph, just a sentence and give thanks for one thing only. It was music to our ears when they began giving thanks to the Lord so we all could join in.

One day the phone rang with a request that we give blood for a crisis in the community. A neighbor a few blocks away had been in a car accident nine months before. Since the accident he had been in a coma in a Philadelphia hospital and was surviving on intravenous feedings and kidney machines and had used 300 pints of blood. We were told that in his delirium he would shout out in anguish, thinking he had killed his son in the accident. No one was able to convince him this was not true, not even a visit by the son himself. I mused, *I know that neither Douglas or myself would qualify medically as blood donors. But I know we can be of prayer help. Though no one has been successful in relieving him of the false guilt he is feeling, God can break through with the truth, even through those levels of unconsciousness. And I must go and talk to the wife who is coping with their five children, all 12 years old and under.*

We visited with this young mother whom we had not met before. We discovered that she was already starting to make funeral arrangements though she had also requested prayer from her Roman Catholic connections. We tried to comfort her by sharing with her that not only we, but our Koinonia group would also be praying for God to do a miracle.

We knew this was a huge hurdle of faith for our Koinonia group but they felt compassion and agreed to make this urgent need a prayer project. Then some voices of doubt whispered into my mind, *You better get some real prayer warriors to help you, some who have moved mountains in faith.* We called several not only to pray for this patient in the hospital but for our prayer group which we imagined was weak in faith. The dichotomy of my own prayer condition didn't occur to me just then. I knew full well the power of our miracle-working God but there was obviously a degree of fear because of my need to rely on others for support.

Within a week we had an unexpected call from the wife, her voice high-pitched with excitement. "The doctor in Philadelphia called me and said that they had another patient who was in need of the kidney machine so they disconnected the one my husband was on. Suddenly his kidneys began to work on their own. Then he woke up, sat up and asked for steak and French fries. I can't believe it! They say it is making medical history!"

One of our group along with Douglas and myself, the wife and some of the children drove to Philadelphia to see this miracle that had come to pass. There he sat, alert and cheerful, though facing future surgeries for broken bones which he had been in no condition to undergo in his comatose state. We were dazed, not by doubts, for we saw the living miracle with our own eyes. Dazed in wonder at a God who hears our quivering prayers, sees our fragile faith, yet chooses to honor those who trust Him by intervening and baffling the medical profession.

The next Sunday at Church I met one of our Koinonia group friends in the hallway, shaking his head in awe, saying, "It sure helps your faith! It sure helps your faith!"

In the book of James, the brother of Jesus writes, "You do not have because you do not ask God" (James 4:2). Jesus himself told his disciples, "Ask and it will be given to you. . .how much more will your Father in heaven give good gifts to those who ask him!" (Matthew 7:7,11).

I reflect on the magnanimous kindness of our loving and compassionate God and ask myself a question: *How many spiritual riches and treasures of wisdom have I been deprived of because my Heavenly Father was waiting for me to ask?*

DOWN BUT NOT DEFEATED

A much-respected, veteran missionary, Mrs. Owens, invited me to accompany her on a visit to a sick Chinese lady. This invalid, Christiana Tsai, had been an influential woman of wealth before being struck down with illness. At this time she had been nearly 25 years bedridden, and I eagerly looked forward to the privilege of bringing comfort to one of God's faithful, suffering servants. I could not imagine the endurance required to face pain and confinement for so long.

As a young mother I didn't feel I had any visitation wisdom or skills to offer. But I was willing to try to walk in the shadow of this missionary giant of faith and bring encouragement to a suffering soul.

We entered this old home near Lancaster, Pennsylvania, and were asked to be quiet. Christiana Tsai suffered from a rare form of malaria which had left her hypersensitive to sound and light. At times she had high fevers and pain, but she could accept us for a short visit this day. We were ushered into a dark room, which had thick curtains to keep out the daylight and a dark cloth covering the only lamp. The room felt heavy, dreary and the old furniture had left its glory in the past. *How depressing. There is no color, not a ray of light, no music, no flowers, nothing to bring cheer to a visitor, let alone the patient.*

As we approached her, this little lady sat straight up in bed as if she had been raised from the dead. Dark glasses covered her eyes but the spiritual sparkle of her spirit vibrated to our hearts. We listened in awe as she spoke of the Lord in scintillating conversation that stunned us into silence. She reigned like a Queen in the Dark with her King of Light.

We felt our spirits lifted and challenged as we observed the zeal of one who loved the Lord and who stirred us to be witnesses for Him wherever we went. In the past she had a ministry to the military in China; now many officials, who visited the United States, formed a parade to visit this saint, weak in body but strong in spirit. She introduced Jesus Christ to many who left with a new allegiance to their new Commander, the Lord of all.

How strange that we have been the ones to be encouraged. I feel so unworthy, so humbled by what I have seen today. With what authority and power she spoke because of the Light within her. I thought we would minister comfort to her but she has ministered a whole new dimension of courage and strength to us. God's strength in human weakness.

Sometimes our days become dreary and our souls feel weary. Then God sends an angel of light, one of His own who has fought and won in the dark battle of despair. Like a Light beaming, the message of one's testimony declares: "Though I sit in darkness, the LORD will be my light" (Micah 7:8).

And we catch a glimpse of heavenly glory.

GRACE FOR GRIEF — Part 1

My mother was visiting us when we heard the terrible news. A young missionary, who had lost one infant in a stillborn birth, had just lost her second newborn. The horror of the double tragedy gripped me as I thought of the baby I was carrying in my womb. I blurted out in anguish, "Mother, I could never go through anything like that." Quietly my mother calmed my troubled heart. "Margaret, as Spurgeon says, 'God gives dying grace for dying need.'" I couldn't answer but I thought, *Yes, I know God has promised grace in time of need but right now I know I don't have the faith to face such sorrow.*

Our neighborhood in Bethlehem, Pennsylvania, was largely made up of young families. One day the pleasant sound of children's voices was drowned out by the wailing siren of an ambulance. It stopped just around the corner from us. Word quickly spread — a baby in that house had died. The news, like a bolt of lightening, struck me with alarm. *Suppose it had been one of my children? Is death that close, that sudden? I feel like gathering all my children around me like a mother hen. I want to protect them.* I was so distraught by this awful intrusion into our happy neighborhood that I had to call Douglas at Lehigh University for comfort. *Clearly I am no saint. My faith doesn't even rise to cope with someone else's emergency. Suppose it was my family that had been hit? I am trying to handle life, but I cannot handle death.*

This incident prompted us to start looking for a supportive church family in our new community. We had just come from a small mission church in New Haven, but we felt strangely drawn to the big and prosperous First Presbyterian Church of Bethlehem. We immediately felt out of our class there, especially after we were ushered out of a pew which had been reserved for Eugene Grace, the multimillionaire president of Bethlehem Steel Co. *Surely this liberal, wealthy Church is not for us*, I thought. Yet after much prayer and despite some misgivings, we believed we were to join that congregation.

Some time later we were invited to speak to an adult group of our Church. It was an unexpected opportunity, and we felt we needed to make the most of it. I scanned the membership list: *They are lovely people and look like they have it all together. But where are they spiritually? They certainly hear stimulating sermons each Sunday. Have they really grasped the simple gospel message? Do they know what it means to have a personal relationship with Jesus Christ?*

On the one hand I felt intimidated to speak before this sophisticated audience. Their education and professionalism was more advanced than mine. On the other hand I felt an inward pressure of responsibility. *This is a unique opportunity to share our faith and encourage them in a simple trust in Jesus.*

Knowing that prayer is the most important preparation for any message we give, I found a quiet place to pray. With a blend of human anxiety and spiritual fervor I poured out my heart to the Lord. *"Please Lord, give me courage to speak your Word, to show these people what it really means to commit their lives to you."* As I thought about it, my prayer became more intense as I pleaded, *"Lord, O Lord, make me a blessing."*

At that moment I heard the inner voice respond, "Are you willing at any cost to be a blessing?" Without hesitation I replied, *"Yes! At any cost, Lord."*

The voice spoke again in a question, "Are you willing to be a blessing at the cost of a child?" Immediately I blurted out, *"No, Lord."*

Silence.

The conversation stopped and I was alone with my thoughts. *What can I do? Well, I'll just have to get through this talk on my own somehow. . .I can get through this immediate assignment, but how can I go through the rest of my life without the Lord? I have blocked Him out. I have sent Him away.*

Silence. I began to reflect on the Heavenly Father I knew. *He has always been loving and kind, someone I could trust. He showed His love all the way to His death. Our children are gifts from God—not ours to own but love loans from the Lord. Doesn't God love our children even more than we parents do?* Surely I should trust them to Him now. I paused to think what it all meant.

Quietly I told Him, *"Yes, Lord, I am willing."*

King David wrote prophetically in Psalm 40:7-8, ". . .It is written about me in the scroll. I desire to do your will, O my God. . ." Jesus in His life revealed that hidden treasure in the midst of costly obedience.

In my own moment of surrender I sensed a holy joy in my spirit and a deep peace in my mind. When I left the room my husband stopped to look at me and observed, "Margaret, your face is radiant." By saying "Yes, Lord," we give Him the key to our hearts and He gives us His Presence.

GRACE FOR GRIEF — Part 2

The invitation to address the Adult Class in our Presbyterian Church became the platform for God to address us. The presentation itself was not necessarily eloquent or memorable, but it was clear that God was preparing us for something. He revealed to us that while we needed courage to meet the challenge to speak, we needed grace for what it would cost to speak His truths with authority.

This was reinforced when we heard the terrible news that a nephew had been diagnosed with Muscular Dystrophy. We felt so inadequate to bring comfort to the family. We tried to write something in a note, quoting significant Scripture verses of hope and comfort. But something was missing. We added a P.S., "We know these promises of God are true though we have never had to prove them with a test like you are going through."

Such a test came for us about a week later. It was summer, and we took our four children – David, 7; John, 5; Paul, 3; and baby Ruth, 18 months — on vacation to Balm Beach on Georgian Bay in Ontario, Canada. My parents, Grandpa and Grandma Seaman, came along with us to relax, swim, read and enjoy the children. We shared a rustic cottage by the water; and we reveled in the simple lifestyle. Chores were reduced to sweeping out the sand once a day. We cooked our food on a two-plate burner and pumped water from the tap in front of the cottage. It had no indoor plumbing but no one minded. It was a special family adventure.

I remember vividly one Monday morning. Paul was throwing pieces of food in the air to the seagulls, laughing with delight as they swept up his morsels. It was a spectacle in the sky with the birds above and the innocent joy of the child below.

Paul's exuberance quickly evaporated the next morning. He did not want his breakfast and was quite willing to lie down in bed. He became nauseated, and we waited for the virus to run its course, but he worsened as the day went on. We became concerned. *He is becoming listless and dehydrated. We have no telephone and it's half an hour's drive into town. Perhaps we should take him to a doctor.*

We were shocked by the doctor's opinion. "I am going to put your son in the hospital. He could have an abdominal obstruction, and we will first try to treat this conservatively. If he needs surgery during the night, we will notify you by the police. There is no need for you to stay in the hospital. We will take care of him."

It hurts to leave a child in hospital but this is the thirteenth hospitalization we have faced in our family and we survived them all. Paul is so lethargic that he wouldn't know whether we were with him or not. Perhaps we should obey the doctor's orders and take care of our other three children at the cottage. We returned to the lake with heavy hearts, but felt assured that we had done the right thing.

The next morning we called the hospital from a telephone booth and asked for a report. I was put on hold, and I could hear voices as if the switchboard was very busy. *Is there an emergency?*

Why are they not answering my questions directly? Why do I have to wait? Don't they know what they are doing? A wave of panic swept over me. I felt trapped in the booth, closed in with fears and no one answering me.

In a flash terror struck me. *If there is a crisis could it be around my child?* I screamed into the phone, "What is happening to my son? I want an answer right now." The answer came, "Both of you come immediately to the hospital."

On our way we braced ourselves in the silence of our own thoughts. Solemnly we broke the silence by prayer: *"Dear Lord, please prepare us for all you are preparing for us."*

We arrived at the hospital and stood waiting while nurses and attendants rushed all around us. *It seems as if we are invisible. Nobody is noticing us and nobody is talking to us. I notice Paul's crib in the corner is flat and I recognize some of these treatment trays the nurses are carrying. They must have had to rush him to the Operating Room. Why doesn't anybody greet us or stop to talk to us? What's wrong?*

Two men in white approached us — the doctor and the Chief of the Hospital. They looked awkward and said it succinctly, "We're sorry. You have lost your son." Immediately I sat down, fearing I might faint. They spoke again, bluntly, "It was just as well you were not here. He died in convulsions. He had encephalitis. You may be grateful that he did not live. He could have been a vegetable if he had survived."

We were ushered to his room to say our farewell to his still body. In shock and sorrow we took in the scene. We held his little hand and kissed his cheek, too numb for tears just then. Like a little bird his soul had taken flight, and we would have to wait before we could see him again.

As we left the hospital the doctors asked if we would like to have some tranquilizers or sleeping pills. We appreciated their attempt to help us through the trauma, but we were already becoming aware of being held together inside. *Is this God's grace in time of need? Is this God, the God of all comfort, at work in me?* We declined the offer of drugs, and as we left the hospital we observed the two doctors standing still, puzzled, watching us in disbelief.

Our first task was to call the family together at the beach. "We took Paul to the hospital and God took him to heaven," we explained. I heard my Mother gasp in shock and then felt the warmth of her arms around me. *I must be strong for the sake of the children. We have things to do. Please Lord keep me from falling apart.* That night we heard the brothers talking to God in their bedtime prayers, *"Dear God, Please tell Paul that we love him and one day we are coming to see him."*

Later they wanted to know how Grandma knew that Paul was going to heaven.

"Grandma didn't know," we replied, "None of us knew."

"Well, then," they asked, "why did she read to us all about heaven?" When we were in the hospital with Paul on his last night on earth, Grandma had picked a Sunday School paper at random and read a story to the other children all about heaven. In such tender ways the little ones were being prepared for what awaited them and our prayer on the road was being answered. I overheard John talking aloud to himself, "I'm sad that Paul isn't here any longer, but I'm glad that he is happy playing on the golden streets in heaven."

Over the next days we walked a path we had never gone before. Neither of us had lost a close relative to death, and we kept wondering if we would be able to handle the demands and decisions. We went back to Toronto to bury our little boy as we had relatives there. *What should we bury him in? He looks as if he is sleeping. Perhaps a new pajama outfit would be appropriate.* In the store we asked for a Size 3. When the clerk asked the age of our son and we told her, she suggested, "You should get a bigger size for him to grow into." Sadly we explained, "We are buying this to bury him in."

At that time, in 1960, the custom was to hold a vigil for three days in the funeral home. The little casket was beautifully framed in flowers and we waited through many hours meeting friends and strangers who came to share their love and condolences. I remember many who came, weeping over words of comfort, their hearts broken in compassion. I pondered, *Isn't this strange? They are weeping over our loss and God seems to be holding us in control, so that we can share the very comfort He is giving us right now. Strangely, that seems to be comforting them in their pain just like their weeping for us, comforts us. Are tears part of God's grace in grief? Alone in the night we waken and weep together. Yet here we sense a serenity to receive our friends and share with them.*

There was a moment when I stood looking at the little casket and marveling that we could converse with all the people around. My soul exclaimed within, *The grace of God — it works!* At that precise moment an elderly missionary approached me with a radiant smile, saying, "The grace of God — it works!" Amazed, I replied, "Brother, we speak the same language!"

God's comfort came to us in many ways. While Douglas waited hour upon hour in the funeral parlor he suffered his own private pain. He recalled one time as a young boy when he was banished to his room in disgrace. His punishment was to memorize a verse of Scripture. Smart and naughty, he quickly returned downstairs able to quote the shortest text in the Bible—"Jesus wept" (John 11:35). His punishment accomplished, he was free! Now the remembrance of that verse washed over his soul in the stark reality of a dead child. This time he was free to cry.

God gave us a unique gift of comfort at the funeral. Dr. Hadjiantoniou, our beloved pastor from Athens, experienced a touching personal moment with Paul shortly before his death. Dr. Hadji — as we affectionately called him – had been on a U.S. speaking tour which included our Church in Bethlehem. Afterward, we dropped him off to his next assignment, but little Paul was distraught at his departure. He cried inconsolably until Dr. Hadji took him up in his arms to comfort him. Then Paul calmly returned to the car. *Whatever happened then? Why did Paul get upset and have to have a farewell hug?*

When he heard of Paul's death, Dr. Hadji came from Detroit to be at the funeral. He arrived just minutes before the casket was closed. It was a profound comfort to us to have this much loved pastor come to see Paul and be with us in that hour. He was the only pastor in Toronto who knew Paul personally. In the homily Dr. Hadji spoke from Mark 10:16: "'And he took the children in his arms, put his hands on them and blessed them.' Mothers long ago brought their little children to Jesus for Him to lay His hands on them and bless them. But Jesus did so much more. He took them up in His arms to bless them.

"These parents, like those mothers long ago, often brought their son to Jesus that He might bless him. And He has done so much more. He took him up in His arms to bless him." We chose those words to be inscribed on the little tombstone. These words have comforted us ever since that sad day.

Letters and cards poured in and the multitude of loving words touched us deeply. We would park in a secluded place to be alone as we read the mail. We suffered waves of grief, but expressions of God's love through his people washed over us like a tidal wave. Overwhelmed, the dam broke and we sobbed in solitude. Those tears, like cleansing comfort, enabled us to return to the cares of the family.

The time came to make the sad journey back to Bethlehem. We treasured our memories, but we missed our child. Life goes on and we had to face its routines again. We came back sobered, but not shaken. I sat on my bed lost in thought, *Could I face the shock of grief like that again? No. I cannot say I have gained in self-confidence. But this I know—I have gained in God-confidence. He does give grace for grief.*

GRACE FOR GRIEF — Part 3

We had prayed for open doors that we could go through to serve the Lord and other people. We had barely unpacked our bags after returning to Bethlehem before our own front door kept opening to welcome visitors and friends. They came to express comfort in many ways.

One of the first visitors was a college professor's wife. She listened only briefly to our story of Paul's death before she spoke words that stunned us. "It is one thing to lose a loved one to God but another thing to lose your husband to his secretary." She was hurting deeply and wanted our support. *Isn't it strange? I thought she came to comfort us but she really needs someone to help bear her heartache. At least we know the God of comfort.* God dramatically answered our prayer for this friend. Her husband was driving to New York with the girlfriend and suddenly came to his senses. He turned around and came back to his family and his marriage.

Another day we received a call from one of our pastors. "Last night the Clerk of Session died of a heart attack and the widow, with her two little children, is distraught. Could you go over and help her?" We found the house crowded with people discussing sports and other topics. *That poor widow. Everyone is talking but she seems left out and even bored. No one wants to discuss the painful subject of her*

79

husband's death. My husband went up to her and asked her how she first met her husband. She grabbed both of us, and ushered us into a private corner to talk about the one closest to her heart. *She seemed so relieved and grateful to have someone to listen to her. Is it because she knows we also have been in sorrow?*

Our community was shocked by the news of a young man in the military who was in a plane which burst into flames and crashed with no survivors. We felt the horror of this tragedy was beyond our capacity to comprehend. *We know the deep pain of losing a very young child suddenly, but this is a son they had known for many years. How do you survive knowing your son was burned alive?* In spite of feeling so inadequate to help these parents we went to visit them. We had nothing to say. We didn't know the young man. We sat in silence and listened to the grieving parents. Our hearts ached for them. After a short time we left thinking, *What comfort could one bring in such stark sorrow?*

In the next day or two, a couple known for their compassion asked us: "What is your secret? After you left those grieving parents, all they could talk about was what your visit meant to them. What did you say? We would like to learn." We could quickly answer, "We felt very insecure and didn't have any counsel or wisdom to give them. We just listened as they talked." A little light was dawning in our souls. *Is the difference because people know we have been there too? We have lost a son and there is a heart empathy in suffering. I also notice that the more comfort we give away, the more my own heart feels comforted. Is sharing God's comfort with others one of the ways He brings healing to our own broken hearts?*

During that first year after Paul's death we became aware of dramatic changes in our lives. We were invited to speak in various churches in Bethlehem and other towns. In Lay Witness missions or Faith at Work retreats in different places, we often found ourselves ministering God's comfort to bereaved people who never had come into healing and wholeness. Some had spent years in the bitterness of their loss, their wounded hearts festering in sorrow.

We also realized how tender our own hearts had become. A little reminder of Paul, like a scribble on the wall, would crack open a reservoir of tears. One time I noticed a little coin in his jacket pocket and a wave of grief came over me. *He was so young to die. Why am I alive and why was he not allowed to live? His little jacket and coin remains—but he is gone. Why?*

One day I was on the telephone and another memory flashed back to haunt me. I had been on the telephone with a friend when I heard Paul downstairs crying and fussing. It took a little while to politely get off the phone so that I could investigate what was wrong. When I did, I found Paul on our bed holding a hurting finger. He had touched the hot iron which I had left to answer the phone. Now I stood by the phone paralyzed, stricken in the grief of regrets. A longing surged through my being to have one more chance to cry my shame of neglect, hug my son, and ask him please to forgive me. *I will never have that chance on earth. How can I ever reach him? I can't go on. This pain is too sharp. It has the sting of sin in it. What can I do?*

Like a tender reminder from the Lord it came to me to talk to Him. I prayed, *"Dear Lord, how much I wish Paul was here so I could ask his forgiveness. Will You forgive me, Lord? And You are the only one who can speak with him now. Would You please tell him how sorry I am and ask him to forgive me?"* The pain was deep and so was the healing. It seemed that all the regrets which are so often the torment of grief, were wrapped in that one incident. I felt forgiven and I never faced regrets again.

About a year after Paul's death Douglas and I were invited to speak at the Girls Pioneer Camp in Ontario, Canada. We told the story of Abraham offering up his son on the altar (Genesis 22) and how that was a picture of God's love, giving up His Son for us. We also shared our own story, experiencing God's comfort in losing a son. After the late meeting we were having a cup of tea in the Director's chalet when the door burst open and a leader shouted, "The leader we've been praying for—she's saved! Hallelujah! She's weeping her heart out, saying that the story of losing your child somehow helped her to see God's love in giving up His Son. At last our prayers have been answered!"

What joy! We left them rejoicing and got in the car to drive back to our cottage. Alone I reflected, *Paul is like a kernel of wheat that has fallen into the ground (John 12:24) and tonight we have seen the fruit of one born into God's family. I remember that prayer when the Lord asked me if I was willing at the cost of a child, to be a blessing. Oh! what a cost! I'm glad someone found Life, but I still wish that Paul was here with us.* It was a moment of truth when I saw the unlimited love of God's sacrifice and the limited measure of my own.

The first Christmas was particularly difficult. Shopping for gifts seemed so superficial. The decorations and tinsel and Christmas carols were out of tune with our mourning hearts. *But I shouldn't feel so depressed. After all, we still have three children. All this holiday cheer is so shallow. Toys and things get broken or lost. What is there to hold on to? What is precious in life that we won't lose? Surely the most precious possessions we have as parents are our children. But we can even lose a child.*

At dark moments of deep searching the Holy Spirit, like a Comforter, leads us to the light of God's Word. The words of Proverbs 10:22 brought hope to us: "The blessing of the LORD brings wealth, and he adds no trouble to it." The blessing of the Lord was something to seek, something to keep and never lose. We were in no mood to send commercial cards to our friends and yet we wanted to communicate with many who had meant so much to us during these grieving months. We created little scrolls and wrote the words of Proverbs 10:22 in calligraphy on manuscript paper. The response we received so warmed our hearts that for 25 years we made our own cards, choosing a Scriptural theme as a message to our friends each Christmas.

A few years later we were back in Toronto on the occasion of my Mother's death. I was asked to speak to a group in an Episcopal Church and shared about the sorrow and the comfort of God in the death of our son. In the group were some refugees known as "displaced people." They were the victims of World War II and had left all they owned and loved in Europe to start a new life in Canada.

After my message a lady came up to me brimming with tears yet radiant with joy, "Oh thank you," she said, "I am a doctor from Hungary, and my husband and I have been so depressed and sad because we left our property and professional life to come to this place. We have felt such a loss, so lonely and sad. But tonight I have hope. I see that God can transform a cup of bitterness into a cup of blessing!"

That night, the night of my Mother's funeral, I could not sleep for joy, an inward joy.

We had prayed for an open door for service and it was our own front door God opened. Because our hearts were opened by being broken, we now could enter into the griefs and sorrows of others with compassion, suffering with them in love. In love's service only wounded soldiers can serve.

We discovered another secret. A cup of bitterness and tears and sorrow is always measured. If we give it back to the Lord He transforms that cup into the wine of His blessing—a cup of joy that overflows.

DUSTERS, DIAPERS AND DISHES

It didn't happen suddenly. It wasn't a major crisis. It was a gradual pervasive awareness that life was boring in the relentlessness of the daily round of routines. Something was not quite right, but I did not know what it was nor what to do about it. God had blessed me with a home I had not asked for, a husband who was a wonderful answer to prayer and dear children, the desires of their parents' hearts. I felt ashamed and guilty that my idyllic setting was not satisfying. My dreams of a professional nursing career had become reduced to the daily demands of dusters, diapers and dishes.

With best intentions I analyzed my situation and rationalized a good solution. Clearly I was an overworked mother who needed a break to get away from the baby and floor and sink level of life. As an answer to my need I felt God provided kind friends who not only took me out for short trips and recreation, but gave these as paid-for gifts while my husband babysat the children. What fun times we enjoyed! *How good the Lord is*, I thought. It was exciting to leave the house and feel like a bird escaping the nest.

Another awareness crept up in me. These happy times were short-lived. As soon as I entered the house the old chores choked the joy out of me and the dull routines faced me again. Oh yes, I did my work faithfully out of a sense of duty, but it was all so unrewarding. I cleaned house because I knew I should. I was glad that my husband, Douglas, gave me the freedom to plan my own schedule and did not pressure me about my work. But then, neither did he notice when I did clean the house. *Who cared or appreciated my labors?*

Then the Lord spoke to me right in the middle of the living room floor as I was mulling over my murmuring thoughts. I heard Him say, "You are rebelling against me." His words shocked me and I immediately dialogued with Him. "Not so, Lord. I am not rebelling against You. You know how devout I am, going to Church, tithing, praying, reading the Bible. . .I am a believer, not a rebel!" He did not seem to answer my response. Worse, my defense gave me no peace.

After an awkward silence I dared to ask, "How am I rebelling against You, Lord?" His answer came, "You are not content in the corner of the vineyard where I have placed you for this season." It was true. My thoughts roamed on. *My tasks are so menial, repetitive and unimportant. Most of what I do is unseen. Does God really care or notice?*

He seemed to flash a picture in response to my question. I saw Jesus with a towel washing the feet of the disciples just hours before He was to be arrested. This would be the memory those disciples would often replay as they recalled His last words and actions among them. I pondered the scene. *Jesus, the very Son of God, taking a towel in His hands to wash dirty feet. How could I resent taking a towel to dry dishes?*

Jesus pleased God in all He did. Jesus was both teaching and showing the disciples how to live and serve God humbly. This was service to God. I remembered the words of St. Paul in

Colossians 3:23-24: "Whatever you do, work at it with all your heart, as working for the Lord, not for men, since you know that you will receive an inheritance from the Lord as a reward."

Slowly those words brought a new perspective. What matters is *who* we are working for, not the magnitude of the task. I began to see the significance of the small as long as it was "work for the Lord." And there was even the promise of a reward!

Hanging up diapers on the line did not become exciting nor did washing hundreds of dishes every week. But something changed inside *me* and I was no longer tempted to "despise the day of small things" (Zechariah 4:10).

In a heart seeking to please the Lord, even trifles become hidden treasures.

SWEET SORROW

Pain. Sorrow. Offense. Betrayal. Some experiences of life can easily harden us. They also can point up the desperate need we have for more of God's grace.

As we mourned the loss of our three-year-old son, Paul, the healing grace of God's comfort took away some of our pain. But only a year later a broken relationship brought not only sorrow, but sorrow with a sting to it. As the apostle Paul said, "The sting of death is sin" (1 Corinthians 15:56). Our son Paul's death was without a sting. A broken relationship has the sin of discord and unforgiveness, hurt pride or jealousy. I felt the ground of my heart crushed by this form of sorrow.

This was the way God prepared my heart for a deep desire and hunger for more of Him. I felt dry and soul-thirsty for the greater Presence and the power of the Holy Spirit. I had an awareness of my spiritual poverty in spite of trusting the Lord and longing to please Him. I wanted to forgive but emotionally all I felt were wounds that hurt. I pleaded with the Lord in intense prayer.

Others had prayed for me and with me to receive more of the Holy Spirit but I felt blocked. Having seen one friend transformed by a fresh filling of the Holy Spirit, I yearned to come into that same blessing. She had a new love for the Lord Jesus and was aglow with joy. *O Lord, please soften the hard ground of my heart.*

His answer came in a quite unexpected way. That summer of 1964 our family went down to Florida for a six-week vacation. The beach, the relaxed atmosphere, the sweet mangoes from the back yard, and family activities like our evening outing to see a magnificent night-blooming cyrrhius delighted us all. But amid this happy time I developed an obsessive fear that one of the children might drown. *Am I still not healed from the death of Paul? We were on a vacation by a lake in Canada when Paul died. Here we are by the ocean. Is that the cause of this terrible fear?* It so happened that our eight-year-old son, John, did nearly drown that summer. A man out swimming found a young boy floundering at his feet and mercifully carried him to shore. It turned out to be John, who had been snorkeling and become disoriented.

This incident prompted me to cry out to God again. *Lord, I should love You and I want to love You but I don't feel love for You. I am so poor in my spirit that I need a gift of Your love in order to have some love to give back to You. Please fill my empty heart with Your Spirit of love.*

While in the Fort Lauderdale area, I started attending a Bible study group led by a godly woman named Grace Munsey. By their comments and questions, I quickly figured some of the participants to be new believers. In one of our meetings, a strong impression came to me. *Ask this group to pray for you.* I looked around at the women gathered there and thought, *Why should these people pray for me? They seem less mature and informed in the Bible than I am.* As I wrestled with my pride I thought of Naaman who nearly missed his healing from leprosy because of his pride (2 Kings 5). *I don't want to be like Naaman. . .I don't want to miss God's blessing.*

They asked me to sit on a chair and gathered around to pray. The leader asked me, "Do you want us to pray that you will receive the Holy Spirit?" I replied, "No, I have received the Holy Spirit but I want to be filled with the Holy Spirit." Grace heeded my request and began to pray. "Now lift up your hands and praise the Lord," she instructed me. *That is not my Presbyterian way. Why do I have to raise my arms up in the air? Well, I don't want to miss the blessing.* . .So I lifted my arms in uncomfortable obedience.

At that moment, Grace's husband in the back of the room began to sing a familiar hymn:

> *Have thine own way, Lord, have thine own way.*
> *Thou art the Potter, I am the clay;*
> *Make me and mold me after thy will,*
> *While I am waiting, yielded and still.*

I tried to yield and be still but I was not aware of anything happening. Grace then gave me a word of wisdom I have treasured through the years, "Don't plead with the Lord anymore. Begin receiving His gift by faith with thanksgiving."

A day or two later Douglas took the four children to the beach to allow me to rest. I had been lying on the bed praying and got up to get my Bible when I sensed the Lord saying, "Be still and rest. Be still." As I waited silently in His Presence, a gentle flow of unknown words began rising up from deep within me, bringing a strange warmth and joy that filled my being.

When Douglas returned from the beach I couldn't wait to share with him how God had touched me. "He has given me a new language, the gift of tongues." My husband was threatened by this event, fearing it would pull us apart and we would no longer travel together on the same path in our spiritual pilgrimage. His countenance was ugly with anger and anxiety. Knowing how truly I had been blessed, I responded only in love. It was then my husband knew something wonderful and genuine had happened to me and within a few weeks, received the gift himself.

The desire to know God and love Him deeply is a grace-gift from Him. In ways we may not understand or recognize He stirs our hearts to hunger and thirst for more of Him. He is waiting to fulfil our desires and to quench our thirst, waiting for us to wait for Him.

Yielded in Love's Presence we are healed from sorrows, filled with forgiving love for those who wound us and free from fear.

OVERCOMING OBSTACLES

There comes a time when every house needs a coat of paint. In our home we made it a family project and we ended up painting ourselves as well as the walls. Our boys, who were quite small at the time, thrived amid the messy days of painting. I did not. It took me several weeks to recover from the pressure of pushing a project in the midst of a house in disorder.

In the midst of our two-week project I noticed again the different ways Douglas and I viewed a task such as this. I used to say, "He sees the forest but not the trees while I see the trees but not the forest." In our painting job, he loved to do the broad sweeps to quickly cover the large open spaces. Meanwhile, I labored long at the window frames and other details. In his painting, Douglas might choose to omit hard-to-reach places or spots that weren't clearly visible. He didn't like ladders so he could easily rationalize missing a spot or two on the ceiling.

Function not *finesse* was his philosophy and standard. If it didn't look perfect he would comfort himself and others by commenting, "Well, that's taken the curse out of it!" It might not look beautiful, but at least it was workable.

By the time we finished painting our little ranch home on Primrose Lane in Bethlehem, Pennsylvania, I was totally exhausted. After all the difficulties of the job, I dreaded the thought of ever having to do it again. But about ten years later, I started thinking about it. Each time I looked around the house I felt an inner warning. *Get ready for another paint job.* I tried to push the thought away, but like shifting furniture in a small space, it was never quite out of sight or out of mind. Eventually I faced reality on two fronts: the house had to be painted and I did not have the emotional or physical energy to cope with it. The only solution was to have it done professionally. I was fully aware our budget would not permit it, but the importance of the issue gave me the courage to ask Douglas if we could hire a painter. "Oh no!" he quickly replied, "I'll do it!" That meant *so would I!*

I shared my anxiety with my prayer partner explaining our need to get the house painted, my husband's response, and my inability to cope with the thought of trying to do it on our own. As I poured out my heart to her I suddenly remembered a quote from Hudson Taylor, the founder of the China Inland Mission. *Move man by God through prayer alone.*

"It seems to me that we could pray that God would move Douglas!" As a quick afterthought I added, "At least I think I am on the right track though it's possible that God might want to move me!" We prayed with all sincerity and fervency.

A day or two later Douglas walked through the kitchen door and surprised me by saying, "Margaret, you can get an estimate for the painting job." *That is the thin edge of the wedge,* I thought. *Is this the answer to our prayer?* I immediately arranged for the painter to come and give us an estimate. This man — a member of our Church named Mr.

DeVries — was a Dutchman with a reputation as the best painter in town. The day came for Mr. DeVries to look over our house and with a degree of nonchalance I pointed out the kitchen and cabinets, the living room and one bedroom. As a bonus consideration I showed him the boys' room explaining, "This room isn't as necessary, but it would be nice." Then we sat down for the moment of truth — the dollars and cents.

Mr. DeVries began, "I am going to offer something that you will not be permitted to refuse. I have heard about the work you do for the Lord and He has blessed me in my work, too. I have wondered why it has taken you so long to ask me, but now you have done so. You buy the paint and let me choose the time and I will paint the whole house as a gift!" I sat stunned in joyful disbelief. Out of the corner of my eye I noticed our son David doing his homework and listening to the conversation. With a wide grin he shook his head in awe and amazement.

Sometimes we struggle to do what we ought or we worry because we can't. Is it possible that God is waiting beside us, waiting for us to give up our self-effort, so that He can say, as He does at the Cross, "Let me do it."

RELUCTANT RECEIVERS

The joy of giving is a significant part of the joy of living. We were soon to discover the joys of receiving, although reluctantly.

As a missionary kid I felt I had been trained to receive gifts of charity from others. I could wear someone else's dress without chagrin, but it was different with my husband, Douglas. He had grown up in a family where his father not only supported his family of six but others also during the Depression in Canada. He was able to afford a maid to help in the house and, being in General Motors, drove a new car each year.

One day an executive from Bethlehem Steel left an unwanted package at our home. When Douglas discovered it was a hand-me-down coat he was adamant that he would not accept it "unless it really fits me." He was counting on the probability that it wouldn't. But it did. Perfectly. He covered his pride in a handsome coat and tried to be thankful. I was rejoicing as keeper of the family budget.

Another test awaited me. It came as a complete surprise when our Koinonia group was having a barbecue picnic. This same executive began to make a speech of appreciation and presented us with FIVE HUNDRED DOLLARS. I was struck silent. *Is this real? It reminds me of the paper money in the game of Monopoly. I've never seen a bill this big. Is this a joke?*

Still overwhelmed by the magnitude of the gift, I could barely focus on the rest of the executive's speech, "We recognize that you have the message and we have the means and we want to be part of the team. We want you to buy a dryer and use the rest for your opportunities to speak and travel." I murmured in my soul, *But I don't need a dryer. I've brought up five babies through the diaper stage, drying the cloth diapers on the lines in the back yard, I don't need a dryer. But I've got to show some gratitude. What can I say? How can we accept such a big gift?*

I started forth in a bold attempt to be gracious, "Thank you very much for this generous gift. We're overwhelmed. We don't know how to accept it, but we'll pray and ask the Lord how He would like us to spend it."

At the end of the picnic our executive friend sidled up to Douglas and whispered in his ear, "This gift is for you, for you personally. It is not for you to write checks out to missions and missionaries." When my husband told me about this restriction my heart leapt in judgment, *What ungodly advice! Nice intention but naughty thought!*

Our first decision was to open an account where we would deposit this gift and call it "The Lord's Account." We would use it for babysitter costs when we went to speak in other places. But deep down, I felt a degree of conscience about that dryer. *Shouldn't I honor the intention of the donors?* Eventually I called my prayer-partner friend, Katie Kricks, and asked her to help me shop for one. Ever practical, Katie led me to a store where they had these machines on sale but it was a deluxe model. I protested, "But I don't need a deluxe model. All I need is the cheapest and simplest model there is." I was quite unprepared for my friend's rebuke, "But Margaret, if the Lord wants to give you a deluxe model, wouldn't you accept it?" Yes. And I did. Then in the days that followed I discovered how much time and energy were saved by that helpful gift.

The phone rang and it was our pastor Lloyd Ogilvie, "There is a conference in Bermuda and one of the speakers has had to cancel. Would Douglas be able to take his place? We would like to invite both of you for the week. You would be guests of the conference during the week. I know you would have airfare expense but just this morning a friend in Chicago gave me a donation to be used for ministries like this. This gift will take care of your airfare but that still leaves your babysitting expenses for a week."

I could hardly wait to tell him that we'd been given a big gift to be used to cover babysitting and other needs for ministries like this. Our family had been blessed to find a devout, elderly Czechoslovakian lady who loved to babysit. Mrs. Slabey's husband was a pastor from eastern Europe and, as an intellectual, spent his time in research and study. Mrs. Slabey grasped the opportunity to serve in practical and loving ways. Our children loved her and, once they were in bed, she poked around the house looking for more work to do. I would come home to polished pots and pans and always, good reports.

We returned from a marvelous week in Bermuda, and we wrote out our check from "The Lord's Account" to Mrs. Slabey for $75.00 for the week. When the check cleared the bank we noticed that Mrs. Slabey chose to use her babysitting money for missions. She endorsed the check with the words, "Pay to the order of the China Inland Mission." She said it was her pleasure to give to the Lord's work and liked to earn the money to give it away. All the babysitting checks made to her were sent to missions.

In spite of the restrictions that generous dona-tion in the Lord's Account has had double value — spent for ministry and for missions.

The apostle Paul told the Philippian Church that he had "learned the secret of being content. . .whether living in plenty or in want" (Philippians 4:12). We know the Lord loves a cheerful giver. I believe, too, that He loves a gracious and generous receiver. Slowly we learn that the fellowship of "giving and receiving" is a gift of double grace from the Lord (Philippians 4:15).

FALSE MEDITATION

The pastor of our First Presbyterian Church personally challenged us to be part of a Faith-at-Work ministry that was developing in our area. The ministry involved visiting churches for weekend conferences, where our Faith-at-Work teams eagerly shared their faith in small group settings. These men and women witnessed boldly about how the Lord brought renewal to their lives, telling radical stories of conversions and answered prayer. Their enthusiasm of joy and love for Jesus often ignited sparks of hope in disillusioned and tired Church members.

We were honored to be invited to join a Faith-at-Work team going to an Episcopal Church in Pittsburgh. But the pressure of our own family commitments soon caused us to doubt the wisdom of getting personally involved. I finally asked , *Lord, we want to serve You with all of our heart and all of our time, but aren't our schedules full enough? This would mean leaving our children for a weekend. Are they not our first responsibility? Besides, we have just started toilet-training the baby and wouldn't our absence traumatize him and mess up his progress?*

We prayed and struggled over the decision. We respected the Faith-at-Work movement but we were also concerned that we wouldn't fit into their exuberant ministry style of telling personal experiences. We were more comfortable in home Bible studies and prayer fellowships.

Finally we decided to make a deal with God. We told Him we would go this one time but not commit yet to future conferences until He confirmed the rightness of this move in two ways: *First, let it be very apparent that You led us there by letting us see some spiritual fruit. Second, let us see that our children are not negatively affected by our absence, in particular, the baby's toilet-training process.* We left the children safely in the hands of a reliable babysitter and went on our way to Pittsburgh.

The team of 40 men and women lined up in front of the rectory as we were greeted by team leader Bruce Larson. The lady in front of me – a woman from Alabama — approached Bruce with a wrap-around bear-hug, exploding with high-pitched excitement, "How are you, Bruce! Hallelu-jah! Isn't it great to be here?" I followed in my rigid reserve thinking, *That kind of effusive emotionalism is not me. I'm not even sure I belong with a group like this.* Bruce in his gracious sensitivity must have sized me up immediately. He put out his hand and gave me a proper, respectful British handshake!

We assembled in the rectory and were offered cocktails before dinner. *What? Does this group drink alcoholic beverages? What kind of church ministry is this?* As we were introduced to each other I was impressed by the warmth and welcome we were given. They were friendly people, and I kept my thoughts to myself. *There are enough of us here that I will get through the weekend and somehow avoid Miss Alabama. I'm culturally incompatible with her.*

Church members and the team all met in a large hall for dinner. Across from us a couple began sharing their sense of spiritual need. In no time we were engaged in sharing the simple gospel of Jesus

Christ. It was evident that this couple was wasting no time in expressing their longing for a personal relationship with the Lord. It was awkward during the meal to pray the prayer of commitment, and we were scheduled to go immediately to another meeting. We alerted Bruce Larson of the situation, and he took this couple to a quiet corner to talk further. In a few minutes they were in prayer giving their lives to Jesus. *Lord, You have answered our first prayer request. Surely you planted us right here to be a witness and to see You at work.*

We started the day early on Saturday, knowing we would have lots of opportunities to share our faith and our joy in the Lord. In my morning Quiet Time I read Psalm 19:14, "Let the words of my mouth. . .be acceptable in Thy sight. . ." (KJV) *O Lord, I'll be talking about You all day! Make me an effective witness.* Then I read again and noticed, "And the meditation of my heart. . .be acceptable in Thy sight. . ." I knew the meditation of my heart was certainly not acceptable to the Lord. In a critical and unloving way I had decided to have nothing to do with Miss Alabama. That made a break in the unity of the team in God's sight.

I faced my sinful attitude and asked forgiveness. I still hoped we wouldn't need to cross paths. It is one thing to ask forgiveness from the Lord; it is another thing to love one another and genuinely express it.

At our morning planning session our whole team met to be given our day's assignments. Bruce announced that newcomers were not given leadership roles but, due to some unexpected circumstance, he needed to ask me to be a leader. I could hardly believe his next words. He asked me to team up with Miss Alabama for a workshop on prayer that afternoon. I felt trapped. *It is do or die. I've got to go through with it. And we have meetings all day so we will have to do it without any preparation. O Lord, help!*

As the workshop on prayer got launched I noticed several things about Miss Alabama. She spoke in a very contemporary way, using slang and not-quite-correct English. She spoke a few words and then passed the ball to me for my comments in my proper British accent. Back and forth we went, taking our turn to speak, like a smooth game of tennis. The more I listened to her speak, the more impressed I became that this lady really knew the Lord and had a prayer life that was perhaps more real than mine.

The next shock was to learn that this praying woman smoked! *How can you be so spiritual and smoke at the same time?* The final jolt was to discover she spoke in tongues. *How could she be filled with the Spirit, be a holy-roller who speaks in tongues and smoke all at the same time?* Yet the more I heard her speak, the more I felt humbled by her intimate knowledge of prayer and love for her Lord.

In spite of my doubts and judgmental spirit, the Lord blessed that workshop. In God's grace and kindness He enabled us to flow together sharing the truths of God's Word. I still look back on that occasion as a high point in my ministry.

When we returned home to our children after this weekend, I almost felt chagrined by the babysitter's report. Far from being traumatized by our separation, the children all had a great time. Even the baby's toilet-training continued without a hitch. *I'm glad all went well, but it would have been nice to hear that they missed us a little bit! The most important thing is that God answered our prayer — more than we hoped for!*

About two years later we were in New York City attending another Faith-at-Work conference. Standing out in the crowded meeting was a familiar face. Miss Alabama! Like old friends we warmly embraced and talked about what changes God had brought into our lives in the last two years. We each discovered God had been at work. She no longer smoked and I spoke in tongues!

God's ways and thoughts are far from our own. We may think He is looking for our service, when He is looking for the *spirit* of that service. We focus on the work of our hands or the words of our mouth, but He listens to the meditations of our hearts.

DRIVING BY FAITH

It was exciting news for the family. Douglas was given a sabbatical year to research a book on ancient Greek music at the Center for Hellenic Studies in Washington, D.C. We would be leaving our little town of Bethlehem, PA, to go to the big city. There we would live in an academic compound in the Georgetown area and spend each weekend exploring the rich resources of that city.

There was only one problem, which loomed large in the heart of our oldest son, David. This was the year he was eligible to get his driver's license. Exercising fear rather than faith, my husband and I felt the risks of learning in heavy traffic in a metropolitan city were too great. We suggested that David wait a year before proceeding with driving lessons. We were thankful and not a little surprised that he acquiesced to our suggestion.

The real driving test came to me that year. Although my husband taught me how to drive, the process was a strain on our marriage. When I was told to put on the brake and inadvertently pressed my foot on the gas pedal, charging with all speed across a train track, our voices and emotions escalated too. Outside the car, on the safety zone of terra firma, we resumed our normal tones and relationship with relief. I always rationalized that I grew up in China riding in rickshaws, which made high-speed traffic an extra pressure point for me.

Eventually my husband's patience and my perseverance enabled me to get my license and assume my share in the family chauffeuring.

In Washington I found myself having to drive our children, along with a neighbor's children, to school on a regular basis. The busy streets scared me and the circles at intersections confused me. In prayer I tried to put the Lord in the driver's seat while my hands steered the wheels. I suspect we were accompanied many times by angelic escort. It was not the setting I would have chosen to gain experience and confidence in driving.

Once the sabbatical year was over, we returned to Bethlehem and it was now David's turn to learn to drive. As was the custom in our family, we made the venture a project of prayer, perhaps motivated by fear as much as faith. I knew only too well the mistakes a learner can make. We expected the process to take many weeks, as it was well known that teenagers often failed the first two or three tests. Imagine our surprise when David passed on his first test! With pride we rejoiced in this answer to prayer — until we suddenly became aware of the next step.

We had never given a thought to the necessity of insurance coverage. Now we faced the increase of $200 to our premium for automobile insurance, a much higher rate than our own premium and a cost we could not afford. It hit like a blow of reality and I found myself saying, "David, we're so glad you got your driver's license, but we can't afford to pay the insurance premium. This means you won't be able to drive for awhile." I felt I had dug a dagger of disappointment into my son. I felt devastated for him and yet desperate in the face of the truth. My sense of sorrow was deepened when I saw his nod of acceptance, his pensive expression and noted his silence from any complaint.

A small voice spoke within, *"Are you trusting in your own resources? Have you asked Me?"* I called David to join me at the kitchen table. I confessed, "David, you know it is true that we cannot pay such a high premium, but we never stopped to ask God about it. If He answered our prayer for you to pass your driver's test, He can make it possible for you to use it. Would you agree to pray with me about it now?" Like two children, a generation apart, learning to live a life of faith, we prayed to our Heavenly Father.

That very day a long-distance call came to my husband from Houghton College. It was an invitation for Douglas to speak at a Roman Banquet the next weekend. There would be an honorarium of $200. We all saw the significance of that timely call.

A strange gift of $30 for David came in the mailbox. It was from a friend who had been discharged from the military for health and emotional reasons. This was followed by another phone call. The friend's mother pleaded with me, "Please tell David to accept my son's gift. My son usually thinks only of himself, and here is one time when he is thinking of someone else. Please do him the favor of accepting his gift." Put in those terms, favor for favor, David was willing to receive the kindness and generosity.

For a third time the phone rang with good news, "I have heard that David has his license and I would like to offer him a regular baby-sitting job on a weekly basis for $5 a week. My children will need to be chauffeured to music lessons, and I wondered if David would be willing to do that?" That was one way he was guaranteed not only to have his driver's license but the car! God not only answered prayer to pass the driver's license test, but built his confidence with the trust to chauffeur children.

Our childhood experiences sometimes strengthen and sometimes hamper our growth in confidence and abilities. I would not have chosen to gain driving confidence in the context of chauffeuring children in the high pressure pace of big city traffic. The Psalmist says, "What man is he that feareth the Lord? Him shall he teach in the way that he shall choose" (Psalm 25:12 KJV).

As little children, young or old, we come to our God and acknowledge a specific need. As our Heavenly Father He comes to us and not only meets that need, but all our needs. Even abundantly above all our needs.

A PARTY — NOT A PUNISHMENT

We were delighted when Douglas was granted a Harvard-sponsored sabbatical year to write a book at the Center for Hellenic Studies located near Georgetown. But our family's move to Washington, DC, in 1968 was culture shock in more ways than one.

Douglas was one of five students, who with their families, were placed in individual houses in an exclusive neighborhood near the Center. Across the road from us lived the Mellon family and similar residences were owned by others in the higher echelons of society. This community had its own brand of exclusiveness which might be described as the sophisticates of the intelligentsia. We formed a kind of academic compound where the heads of the households matched wits at cocktail parties, competed in their intellectual pursuits, dined in the finest of restaurants and all felt part of the privileged elite.

Though our simple-lifestyle family didn't quite fit into this scene, we made friends with our neighbors and sought to present a good witness for Christ. In three weeks I launched a Bible study group for the women who, in this isolated community in the center of Washington, were glad to meet for the discussion.

Our teenaged sons, David and John, were going through culture shock too. When they began attending public school, they found themselves surrounded in a sea of black faces. Both of them made good adjustments, and David introduced some gifted young African-American friends to the all-white Youth Group at Fourth Presbyterian Church where Richard Halverson was the Pastor. (He later became Chaplain of the U.S. Senate).

It was a wonderful, yet turbulent year. Each weekend we visited historic sites, picnicked in parks, toured the Smithsonian Institute or enjoyed the National Gallery of Art. But as we were exploring, Washington and other cities were beset by civil unrest. After the assassinations of Sen. Robert Kennedy and Martin Luther King, there were riots and fires all over the city which left burnt scars of devastation. One happened on the day of David's birthday party and his school friends kept calling that they had no way to get through to the party.

John used to walk through a section of woods to go to his junior high school. One day he was accosted by about eight boys, who demanded, "Give us your money." John felt intimidated and outnumbered, so he handed over his wealth, as he recalls, about five dollars.

We notified the police who took John for a ride around the area to look for these teenagers. John thought he knew them. *If he has to identify them and testify against them, won't that make them even more hostile and vengeful? But how else can they put a stop to this kind of behavior I wonder?* We were almost relieved that they were unable to find them.

At another time David was attacked but not seriously hurt by some boys. As parents we questioned what we should do to prepare our boys for bullies at school or on the road? *What is the right response? Should our sons fight back in defense?*

Should they report misdemeanors or ignore them?
Should they turn the other cheek as Jesus suggested?
(Luke 6:29).

We prayed and a wild thought came to us. *Throw a party!*

Our focus now was planning a menu, sodas and pizza and whatever treats we thought the young teenagers would like. The boys joined in the spirit of doing good to those who hurt them. We all looked forward to the party.

We had not anticipated the reaction of the young boys. John invited them but they peered through the gate of our elite residence and were probably suspicious of the invitation. I recognized that they no doubt felt even less able than we to fit in here. But we encouraged John not to give up and to be friendly when he saw them. We stocked up on snacks that could be served at a moment's notice, not knowing when they would venture through the gate.

Once again these boys approached the gate and almost accepted the invitation to come in, but hesitated. *They seem curious, as if they want to explore this forbidden territory. Do they feel guilty for what they did to John? Do they just lack courage?* We encouraged John to persevere in his invitation.

The day came when about half the boys dared to accept the invitation. Immediately we went into high gear and set the table. One of the boys had a nylon stocking stretched tightly around his head. *Does he have lice? That's what they do when they treat for lice, I know.* We sensed our guests were bewildered and somewhat shy, hardly believing the adventure they were in. As hosts we were all smiles, delighting in their presence, and the opportunity to share hospitality. John took them for a tour around our home as they were interested to see how we lived. At the end, somewhat overwhelmed by what had happened, our guests left us, saying, "Thank you."

We learned again one of God's secrets. To overcome one's own inner enemies of fear and unforgiveness, seek to bless those who offend. It becomes a spiritual party of joy!

GOD'S ANSWER TO MY PRAYER — NO!

The call for parents to volunteer their help in the schools was shocking to me. *Is the situation this desperate in the capitol of our nation? Is the standard so low that they are wanting the help of untrained mothers? Is there not enough in the federal or city education budgets to hire certified teachers?*

Whatever the cause, I needed to respond. The only requirement was a chest X-ray for tuberculosis testing. Before the tests were cleared, I was accepted to act as an aide, helping to supervise the students during homework and assignments when the teacher was absent. It was quite a pleasure to find myself in the classroom of a public school bypassing the rigors of professional studies. I was trained as a nurse and here I was exchanging my nurse's cap for a new career. Until the mailman brought bad news.

The chest X-ray was not satisfactory and needed to be repeated. When the second X-ray was questionable, Douglas determined to put me in the hands of the best doctor he could find. This doctor in the Georgetown area of Washington D.C. repeated the X-rays and soberly gave them to Douglas and myself to look at. Even our untrained eyes could see the dark shadow between the heart and lungs and our educated guess immediately signaled: "Tumor. . .malignant tumor. . ."

The doctor said he had consulted with six other doctors, and they had reluctantly concluded there was only one option open to me — exploratory thoracic surgery. The news was shocking and his last words confirmed the fear of the threat we faced. He had no hope to offer. Rather, with a serious face and solemn tone he hesitatingly suggested, "We must think positively." I thought, *In his mind there is not much positive to think about.*

The following days were spent in preparation for the crisis facing me. Clearly, I only had one source of help and hope. My mind was plagued by the awful possibilities while I sought in my soul to find courage and comfort and even a miracle from God.

A kind friend in Washington gathered an assortment of her friends and arranged for us to have a healing service in an Episcopalian Church. It was a gathering of strangers in a strange place, caring enough to bring someone in need to the Lord for help. I felt strangely comforted as they sang a capella, "The law of the Lord is perfect, converting the soul: the testimony of the Lord is sure, making wise the simple. The statutes of the Lord are right, rejoicing the heart. . . . More to be desired are they than gold" (Psalm 19:7-10, KJV). I felt secure in God and the power of His Word which builds confidence. The doctor's kind attempt to be helpful only stirred up fear.

We talked to praying friends, and we prayed. The battle still raged within my heart. With everything in me I wanted to believe for a miracle and I tried to rise up in faith to receive it. I recall having 25 chest X-rays over those weeks. I remember waiting in the clinic booths of the hospital outpatient department. I was standing on tip-toe inside my heart, waiting to hear, "The X-rays are clear." I asked for that miracle, but God never gave it.

The day for surgery was getting closer and I was getting weary in my struggle of faith. *I wish I could live to raise my children: David, John, Ruth and Peter ranging from 16 to 6 years of age. That is my greatest desire and greatest concern as a mother. But my future is bleak and it will take a miracle of healing at this point.*

While I lay on my bed, I believe the Lord guided my thoughts as I meditated on His Word. *My body is the temple of God, it is His property, not mine. The purpose of the temple is to manifest the glory and presence of God. I want to manifest His glory in a remarkable healing so that others, too, may see and marvel. It would be a documented miracle; the tumor was there and then it disappeared and all would know only God could have removed it.* He has the power and only He would receive the praise.

I continued to muse on: *There are other ways to glorify God. We may glorify Him in life or death, when we belong to Him. It is what Charles Spurgeon called, "Dying grace for dying need." When we accept what the Lord allows, that is a testimony which gives glory to God. Am I willing for a premature death? I may not have the choice, but would I be willing to give that potential choice to Him?*

The last option was the hardest to face. *The worst possibility, the one that frightens me most, is prolonged, painful suffering. I am a coward and I don't want to go through an agonizing death. If I fail in the pressure of that final test I would feel ashamed to disgrace the Lord.*

I was comforted by a glimpse into the suffering of the apostle Paul in Philippians 1:19-21.

He was in prison and facing a threatening, unknown future, wrestling with the ultimates of life and death. He first speaks in confident faith: "I know that through your prayers and the help given by the Spirit of Jesus Christ, what has happened to me will turn out for my deliverance" (Phil.1:19). Perhaps he suddenly questioned whether that deliverance would be out of prison or out of life itself. He went on in courageous and yet cautious faith, "I eagerly expect and hope that I will in no way be ashamed, but will have sufficient courage so that now as always Christ will be exalted in my body, whether by life or by death" (Phil.1:20). So I thought, *Paul wrestled with the same fear of failing in the grace of God and depended on the prayers of others and the help of the Holy Spirit.*

Almost imperceptibly, like the slow dawning of a day, a truth was revealed to me. The temple is God's creation and how He desires to express His glory through it is His choice. My response was to grant Him that choice with a positive statement of faith, "Lord, bring glory to Yourself through the temple of my body in whatever way You choose."

There is no way to describe the peace that permeated my being. All the unknowns still faced me (the doctor warned me stretching my ribs apart would result in rheumatoid-like pain for at least two years), but as I went in for surgery peace reigned in my heart. When I awoke from the anaesthesia the doctors greeted me with good news. "You had no tumor — just two diverticuli of the pericardium, the lining around your heart. It was easy to fix, but a rare condition. Had we known that was the problem we would never have put you through such major surgery."

We did not see the miracle I had prayed for, but even the doctors were surprised that, in spite of an incision half way around my chest, I was scrubbing the floor and almost out of all pain within a month. My non-Christian neighbors commented in wonder about the "peace" which they observed but could not understand. The gold key to that treasure was the Word of God sung in a service, read in the life of Paul's suffering and revealed to me as my own inner heart was physically and spiritually exposed.

Psalm 19 proclaims, "The heavens declare the glory of God" and "The precepts of the Lord are right, giving joy to the heart." I give this peace-offering of joy to the glory of God.

SILVER IN YOUR SACKS

After the adventures of the big city we dreamed of a summer vacationing in Europe while Douglas worked on research. He was confident that he would be given a large fellowship grant that would allow the family to travel with him. But he never heard from the professor at Yale who later confessed with abject apologies that indeed, he would have recommended Douglas for the grant, but the application was lost under the clutter of papers on his desk.

A less remunerative grant was offered and the family prepared for a summer of separation. Douglas was to tour museums in Europe and research ancient musical instruments while the rest of the family returned to our home in Pennsylvania. I was prepared to look after Ruth, 10, and Peter, 6, but I was concerned about our two teen-aged boys. Mulling over my options, I asked the Lord: *How can I keep them happy and productive during the summer vacation?*

A call from Kenneth Houck, a member of our Church and an executive in the Bethlehem Steel Corporation, complicated my problem. "Would you consider going to Europe with your husband? My wife and I want to take care of Ruth and Peter for the time you are away, and we will insist that you accept our offer as a gift. No reimbursements or appreciation gifts!" *How can I resist such a fabu-*

lous offer? But it makes no sense! I still have two teenagers on my hands. How can I graciously decline?

Soon thereafter I got another surprise call. "I have news for you," my friend Katie announced. "Folks I know at Quiet Valley Historic Farm Museum are looking for help. They want two teenaged boys. Would David and John be interested?" It was easy to recognize this as an answer to my worries, if not my prayers. *What a rich experience for the kids. God is good. The boys will appreciate the contrast between the sophistication of historic Washington, DC, and the simple rural life of pioneer peasants from Germany who immigrated to Pennsylvania 200 years ago. Thank you, Lord, for this wonderful offer.*

Two hurdles remained. The round trip fare for me to go to Greece would be $240. It seemed an extravagance for me to spend our meager savings for a mere personal holiday. We needed to save our resources for future expenses and the children's education.

"Lord," I prayed. *"I have no peace about this. True, we do have it in the bank, but is it appropriate to spend the family's savings for Mom to have a vacation trip to Europe? Please confirm the rightness of such a lavish decision."*

Douglas flew out of New York for Athens and on the way, stopped at Rome. He went to the Travel Agency and discovered there was only one seat left on a special charter flight. He snatched the opportunity and booked it for me. It would be a five-week round trip.

Meanwhile, in Bethlehem I received a letter from the hospital in Washington, DC, where I had had major surgery six months before. They informed me that we had overpaid my hospital bill and they were reimbursing us with an enclosed check for $239.50. That evening I shared the story with our fellowship group and asked, incredulously, "Do you think the Lord means for me to go on this trip?" Our friend Ralph Emerson quickly put his hand in his pocket and pulled out a coin, "All you lack is a Kennedy half!" I have kept that 50-cent piece as a precious souvenir.

"But Lord," I argued, *"there are five weeks of expenses. What about the cost of living over there?"* The mailman brought God's answer to that prayer in a letter from the Internal Revenue Service. It read, "You have overpaid your taxes. You may cash the enclosed check for $175." I looked in disbelief. A quick calculation confirmed that the living costs according to our <u>Europe on $5 a Day</u> Travel Guide would be met to the penny! *Did I really make a mistake in the tax calculation? Why would these checks arrive just at this time? Did God have to hold them for me in His bank, so to speak, because He wanted to bless me but knew I would be reluctant to take savings out of the bank for myself?*

Long ago Jacob's sons traveled to Egypt to get food in a time of famine. Unknown to them, their brother Joseph whom they had so cruelly mistreated years before was in charge of the famine relief program. Negotiations were tough, but donkeys were eventually loaded with grain and they returned to their father in Canaan. As they unloaded their provision, to their dismay, they found their purchase money for the grain packed in pouches inside their sacks. They were frightened and Jacob exclaimed, "Everything is against me!"

Later, in dire need they returned to Egypt for more grain, taking double repayment of the silver they had found in their sacks. "Perhaps it was a mistake," sighed Jacob. The story is told in Genesis 42-45.

119

Sacks may represent our varying circumstances and needs at different stages of life's journey. Disappointments and troubles are like empty sacks we carry to God. In His love He fills our sacks with the provision for our need. Later, when we stop to rest and look into situations which have been traumatic or painful, we discover silver in our sacks.

The silver speaks to me of spiritual wisdom and insights, God's riches received as a bonus hidden in the sacks of our experiences. God not only rescues us in our hardships but through them makes us richer in knowing Him and His wonderful ways. We know we are unworthy and might even expect a rebuke for lack of faith or lack of wisdom in the choices we have made. Instead, we are surprised by His kindness, His caring, His generosity.

Like the steward who reassured those unworthy and frightened brothers, we hear Him say, "Its all right. Don't be afraid. Your God, the God of your father, has given you treasure in your sacks" (Genesis 43:23).

REST, RACING AND RECOVERY

Free at last! Free from the house, free from the chores, free from the children. I was on my way to a five-week second honeymoon with my husband in Europe. *Every Mom should have a break like this in the middle of her child-raising years,* I thought.

Douglas met me at the Athens airport and whisked me off to Corinth where we relaxed to the lullabies of the sheep bells as flocks grazed on the surrounding hills. Beyond them on the far horizon was the Aegean Sea, more blue and peaceful than I ever imagined. As I gazed on this pastoral scene I was struck by what a picture of Psalm 23 it was. *Just as David was, we have been led to green pastures and still waters. Soul-restoring rest.*

Douglas gave me a personal tour around the museums among the artifacts of ancient civilizations. Because of my ignorance of these cultures, our wanderings through rows of broken relics was of little interest to me. But I tried hard to listen as Douglas expounded on the finer points of the works of art. I recall one touching moment when his eyes welled in tears. He spoke lovingly, "Margaret, you are learning and entering into my world!" *My dear Douglas,* I mused as I smiled back at him, *I'm not really that interested, but I'm pleased to see that you are moved. I hadn't realized how detached from your work I've been and how absorbed in my own. With all the demands of family and household how could*

I possibly have time to live in your world too - except on vacation like this?

I had five glorious weeks without the complications of busy home schedules and children competing for my attention. It was a time of reflection, a time to sort out priorities. But all too soon it was time to return to Pennsylvania.

Inspired by our refreshing holiday, I determined to start all over again, to do things right. *I'll be the perfect wife and mother and homemaker.* It felt like a crash landing when I awoke to the reality of our home. After five weeks away the lawn needed mowing, the car needed washing, the children needed to be chauffeured, their laundry needing doing and groceries had to be bought. I had one day to get the house ready, and I thought I would please my husband by having everything in order when he arrived back home. With high motivation and the pressure of a deadline I accomplished all the tasks. *I have made a good beginning toward my goal to be a pleasing wife, a perfect mother and a competent homemaker*, I thought.

About that same time, a nagging ache developed in my left shoulder joint. *I guess I overdid it when I worked so hard. But it is not that severe,* I thought. *Perhaps I'm just feeling a general fatigue.*

During the following weeks the pain lingered, but the fellowship group which met weekly in our home for Bible study and prayer began to explode in numbers. People poured in our front door, coming from different churches and neighborhoods. We used to call it "wall-to-wall people" until they eventually began to pray that we would move to a bigger home. There was great excitement as people came seeking more of Jesus in praise and worship, listening to His Word, praying together and receiving healings and gifts in the Holy Spirit. *Why,* I wondered, *does God answer a prayer for healing someone's back when I lay hands on them, yet not heal my shoulder joint? My problem is so small by comparison. Perhaps I should humble myself and ask them to pray for me!* They prayed, but the problem remained.

The day came when I decided I had had enough. The ministry was blessed and the family was doing well and I was hurting. I could not lift my left arm any higher than the level of my shoulder and, after five months, it appeared to be permanently crippled. Something was wrong.

Sitting down on my little rocker I had it out with the Lord. "What are you saying, Lord? I see all these miracles of healing in my house and here I am with a minor problem which is wearing me out. I will not get up from this rocker until You speak to me." I waited, listened and heard one word, "Jacob." *What has Jacob to do with me? Jacob? Did I hear right?*

Searching in the Bible I noticed some parallel problems. Jacob was a schemer and one who grasped for God and His blessings. At one time, in a wrestling match with an angel, his thigh was put out of joint. The last portrait of him is in the gallery of the heroes of the faith (Hebrews 11:20-21). He is seen leaning on the top of his staff, worshiping. *Does that mean that he was never healed? With his thigh out of joint was he still limping? Is this how we learn to cease from our self-efforts and lean on the Lord?*

The more I sat and listened, the more revelation I received and the more uncomfortable I became. *I don't have to strive for perfection in works, but to make every effort to enter into God's soul-rest. God isn't looking for a self-willed strong striver, per-*

forming perfectly, but a strong leaner, resting on Him and taking time to be with Him. My shoulder pain must be from the strain of striving by my own effort and strength.

Isaiah puts it clearly, "In repentance and rest is your salvation, in quietness and trust is your strength, but you would have none of it. You said, 'No, we will flee on horses...' (Isaiah 30:15-16). *"Yes, I have something to learn here. I was racing like a horse to be a perfect wife, mother and homemaker by my own self-appointed standards.* Isaiah continues, "Yet the Lord longs to be gracious to you; He rises to show you compassion" (Isaiah 30:18). *God wants me to wait and listen so that He can tell me what to do to please Him. It is like my husband who was so pleased when I wasn't serving him but just loving him, being with him and listening to him.*

When I finally got out of that rocker, I made a doctor's appointment. I also asked him to pray for me, which he did. To my surprise, he also referred me to an orthopedic surgeon. The doctor's first order to bring healing was to put my arm in a sling. I was forced to rest.

After a few weeks I began to feel a strange gnawing sensation in my left shoulder. At this point the surgeon changed my treatment from resting in a sling to exercising the muscles around my shoulder joint. I had to pull on weights from a pulley set up in the basement and climb the wall with my fingers, reaching higher and higher. Both exercises were painful and frustrating. I mumbled in my thoughts, *Lord, you know what a ridiculous waste of time this is. You could have healed me with a touch. Here am I climbing walls and pulling weights when I should be busy about my work and Your king-dom.* One kind Christian friend sent me a tape of worship music which I played to please her, though it was not my taste of music. While my fingers were working their way up the wall, my feet were tapping to the rhythm of the beat. Soon I could raise my arm all the way to the sound of songs of praise.

The day came for the final visit to the doctor. He looked puzzled as he searched through my records. "Didn't I give you a cortisone shot?" he asked. "No," I replied. He saw that I could lift my arm straight up above my head. "You see," I informed him, "It was God who healed me— not you!" He looked at me kindly, gave me a hearty slap on the back, and exclaimed, "I like your philosophy!"

Sometimes the lessons of truth in God's Word are painful. In Hebrews 5:11-12 we are told that God's Word is something like a surgeon's sharp knife: it separates soul and spirit, joints and marrow. The joints attach muscles representing our self-efforts and soul-strength. The marrow is where life-giving cells are created and speaks of the energy of the Spirit. There is a rhythm in God's order: a time to rest and a time to serve.

Isaiah tells us that God is waiting to show us His love. If we ignore him, racing ahead of Him, He allows adversity and affliction, not to crush us but to conquer us. When we do not wait to listen for His voice, He waits to listen to our cry. It is one way we are drawn back to His love.

We picture Him with tears in His eyes, as He tenderly whispers a secret in our listening ear, *"You have worked so hard, but all I longed for—was you."*

PATMOS REVELATIONS

The Greek islands are like jewels set in the sparkling Aegean Sea, each one with its own unique character and beauty. Douglas and I had the privilege of taking a Greek islands cruise in 1968, and as we hopped from island to island, we delighted in their diversity and history.

On the bare rock island of Delos a statue of Apollo rose above some ancient ruins, a lonely reminder of the days when Delos was a center for the Roman slave trade. On Thera, now known as Santorini, we saw evidence of the greatest volcanic eruption in recorded history. Two-thirds of the island disappeared in the sea when Thera's volcano blew about 1500 BC. On Mykonos we delighted in a lone pelican named Petros, which stood like a guardian on the dock greeting all visitors. While on Rhodes, clouds of colorful butterflies fluttered out of trees and bushes at the call of a whistle.

Of all the islands, however, the one we desired most to visit was Patmos, where the Apostle John received and wrote down the end-times prophecies known as the Book of Revelation. The picturesque and peaceful island had been a place of pain and isolation for John. Yet here in the loneliness of exile God spoke to him and by writing what he saw and heard, we also can hear those words and see those visions.

With great anticipation we disembarked from the *M/V Romantica* and began our trek up a mountain to visit the island's historic monastery. Inside were ancient relics and manuscripts of beautifully hand-written Scriptures that were preserved and displayed by Greek Orthodox monks. We viewed them with awe and reflection until our ship's shrill whistle summoned us back to the wharf. Like all tourists, we had schedules to meet and travel dates to keep. Our guide quickly assigned us to a taxi and told us to ask the driver to stop briefly at the cave where John is believed to have written the Revelation. But fearful of being left behind on this remote island, we rushed for the ship.

We made it in time, but as I settled into my cabin's bunk, I was suddenly hit with the painful realization that we forgot to ask the driver to stop at the cave. *How could we forget? This was our one chance in a lifetime. I can't believe we missed it.*

I sat dejected in discouragement and thought, *Well, if I didn't see the place, at least I could take this time to read what John wrote.* Half-heartedly I picked up the Bible and was taken aback as I read words which spoke right into my heart. "Blessed is the one who reads the words of this prophecy, and blessed are those who hear it and take to heart what is written in it, because the time is near" (Rev.1:3). *It says nothing about blessed are those who see where the words were written.*

We missed the cave, but more importantly, we nearly missed the message. God's great book was in my hand containing pearls of truth. How close I came to throwing them overboard in a moment of despair. It is a privilege to visit significant places related to Biblical history and people.

But, it is a priceless treasure to hold God's words not only in our hand but in our hearts.

The Lord delights in those who love and trust Him. He also delights in giving us the desires of our hearts. We never dreamed that eight years later we would have the privilege of revisiting Greece. Through a generous gift from friends we celebrated our 25th wedding anniversary by taking the family on a Greek Island cruise. This time all of us were able to see Patmos and enter the cave which traditionally is considered the place where John wrote his inspired book.

Patmos is a memory we cherish. But we value far more the eternal truths in the Revelation written there.

A "ROYAL" MOVE

The trustee of the First Presbyterian Church offered me the keys to the Pastor's house but I couldn't accept them. "Please," he said, "We decided at a meeting last night to sell the Manse, and we believe it would be just right for you and Douglas." Friends had been urging and even praying that we would move to a bigger home to accommodate all the people coming to our house for fellowship meetings. I suggested the trustee talk to my husband at the next service. *Hopefully he will forget or Douglas will decline. I'm not ready for a big move.* But when Douglas came home he had the keys of the Manse in his hand.

Later, trying to enjoy a Sunday nap, I tossed on the bed, turning over the options in my mind. Finally, I hopped out of bed and called Douglas, "We better pray about this house. We have to give the trustees an answer."

We dropped to our knees and I prayed, "Dear Lord, we are so uncertain about moving to a bigger house. What do you want us to do? We feel the pressure of people and prayers pushing us to move. Are our doubts like the waves of the sea tossing us back and forth or is it the wind of your Holy Spirit..?" Just then the front door opened and another trustee blew into the house with his coat trailing behind him.

"I don't know why I am here," announced our friend. "I intended to go visiting someone in the Muhlenberg hospital. Oh! I guess I am here to encourage you to consider the Manse. It would be so right for your family. . ."

Over the next few days I continued to wrestle with the decision: *I am quite content to stay in this little home. We are happy here. We are only feeling crowded because of all the other people who come into our home for Bible study and prayer fellowship. This is like a sacred place to me. So many have met the Lord in a special way in this house. I treasure those memories and miracles of God's healings, prophecies, answered prayers. I cherish this first home we ever owned. We lived here when three of our five children were born. "Lord, I don't want to move."*

Waves of grief came over me at times, and at other times waves of doubt. *Lord, you know that we are only just making ends meet in this small house. How can we move to a Dutch Colonial mansion with its four bedrooms, huge living room, big dining room and kitchen, library, nursery, pantry and walk-up attic? We don't have enough furniture to fill it and what we have will look like junk. We'll make that beautiful home into a barn and go bankrupt in the process.*

To settle the financial feasability and perhaps the whole issue of such an absurd purchase we decided to seek financial counseling. We invited a wealthy businessman in our Church, known for his wise and godly counsel, to come over and help us. We expected he would quickly agree that we were not in the market for a house the size of this manse. We laid all our books and papers before him and he examined the figures. When he looked up he exclaimed, "It will be a tight squeeze, but it is possible. Praise God! The Feavers are moving at last!" On that note it sounded more like a prophetic proclamation than a counseling session.

Deep inside I felt a turbulence which nothing resolved. Desperate, I fell on my face to the floor and wept.. *O Lord, you know how I have judged others for coveting bigger homes and trying to compete with neighbors. I thought materialism was their god. Can it be that my home has become my idol? At least they had big idols and here am I worshiping a small idol. In my heart I am the greater sinner.* The revelation stung as the tears streamed down my face.

One afternoon I was resting, reading Brother Andrew's book: <u>God's Smuggler</u>. I came across the section telling how Brother Andrew had been collecting clothes for the poor and always gave the best away. He would keep for his needy family only the unwanted remnants, the drabby leftovers. One day the Lord showed Brother Andrew that he was living like a pauper when he was the child of a King. As kingdom royalty he was to trust God for good gifts and clothe his family in the finest of the apparel provided. Brother Andrew thought he had been sacrificial and unselfish, but the Lord revealed to him a heart that limited God's generosity to those in his own royal family. In a flash of illumination I saw my own heart and broke into deep sobbing. *Lord, I thought it was a mark of spiritual maturity to be content with little. Have I been resisting your generous love? Have I deprived myself and our family because I didn't trust or accept all the good things you wanted to lavish on us? Have I blown away your blessings by my unbelief? How could I have been so wrong?*

We decided to accept the offer to buy the manse and when we called, the trustee immediately dropped the price. Church contractors renovated the bathroom and kitchen for about half the normal price. Friends came from Bethlehem and towns around to repair, decorate, shop, launder, paint and paper. A couple of executives from Bethlehem Steel spent spare evenings painting the basement and varnishing the bannister. Others offered furniture, including a new stove which we had to decline. We had no room for it. I remember our oldest son, David, enthusiastically painting a bedroom with a friend, saying, "This isn't just our house, you know, this is really a fellowship house. It's the Lord's house."

Those weeks people came from all around to help. There was no time schedule or plan so no one was able to coordinate all this volunteer help. But it went well anyway. To our amazement the work was completed the very evening before our move.

In a mystery which I cannot explain in figures, once we moved to this home we never felt the squeeze on our budget again. We opened our door to this bigger house and God sent many more people to fill it, many gifts to furnish it and all we needed to pay for it.

The prophet Jonah was in dark solitary confinement in the stomach of a fish when a revelation came to him: "Those who cling to worthless idols forfeit the grace that could be theirs" (Jonah 2:8). A cherished blessing from God can become an idol in the heart when we cling to it. What was gratitude for a gift can turn into possessiveness that limits the new generosity God's grace wants to give.

When we love and honor the Lord as King, He treats us as royal children. He opens His treasury and opens our eyes. He shows us what His love has prepared beyond anything we have seen, heard or imagined.

THE HEART OF HOSPITALITY

In some ways being brought up in a missionary boarding school was like being raised in an orphanage. The Christian staff were dedicated and loving but our days were organized with almost military precision. We marched to the "drumbeat" of the early rising gong and to bells which meant we were to line up, parade into the dining room, be in the classroom, get into bed. Hired servants did the laundry, mending, cleaning and cooking. We were not permitted in the kitchen so I had never learned how to cook.

Therefore, my dream of being married was slightly shadowed by my fear and ignorance of domestic arts. My fiance, Douglas, kept the romance aglow with his own priorities, "Just feed me love and music — that is all that matters." But I decided one of us needed to be practical so I signed up for a couple of evening courses at the Central Technical School in Toronto in basic sewing and cooking.

In spite of all the motivation needed to learn these skills, I felt at times overwhelmed by the complications of cooking a whole menu to be served at one meal on time. I mused, *How can I be so confused in putting a meal together at night school when I've got the brains to teach nursing science to intelligent students in the day?* I graduated from my cooking course with a gracious "B" which I believe was really earned by my measure of enthusiasm, not performance.

From our earliest married days, my husband was a very kind guinea pig. While I experimented with the help of Betty Crocker's Picture Cook Book, he fed me the encouragement of his appetite and appreciation.

He was so forgiving that I dared to risk his displeasure on a couple of crises some years later. Each day I would make five lunches, one for my husband and one for each of our four school children. Douglas would take his lunch and eat in the newly renovated dining room at Lehigh University. Waiters served in the formal setting of tables arranged with silver on white tablecloths, but style was not important to Douglas. This day his table companion turned out to be the president of the university. As Douglas opened up his bag lunch he discovered two sandwiches made out of four heels of bread, all from different loaves. This was a little embarrassing though he enjoyed his lunch with his distinguished boss. When Douglas received a raise in salary shortly after that, he wondered if the appearance of his lunch had prompted and impressed the president to have mercy on the poor professor.

When this president retired, one day Douglas had the fortune to sit at a table with the new president. It was a privilege to have this opportunity to converse with leaders of the university. When Douglas picked up his bag lunch this day he discovered that the bag got longer and longer as he unfolded it. His wife had clearly run out of lunch bags, and had solved the problem by using a full-sized grocery bag. This time the president was prompted to recall stories of the eccentricities of other Classics professors!

Though it took constant practice to develop competence and confidence in the art of cooking, I loved to try new recipes and offer hospitality. It was a good preparation for the years when we would entertain many people coming to our home for fellowship meals and meetings.

Although our door was usually open, there was one holiday evening when we hoped a big snow storm guaranteed no visitors. I planned a private party for our family alone. With special care I fixed a fancy fondue dinner to be served in the living room around the warmth of the fire. This was to be a rare treat — a family memory for us to cherish.

The door bell rang. *Who could this be? Who would be so crazy as to be out driving on a night like this? I can't believe it.*

It was a pastor from New Jersey bringing a young man from California whom he thought, no doubt, that we would like to meet and help. Protocol demanded that we welcome them into the house, but my heart was wanting to shut them out. *Oh dear! What am I to do? I have just enough portions for the family, how can I stretch the food for two extra men? Why did they have to come this night of all nights?* I scrambled in the kitchen trying to stretch the menu in creative ways while the young man followed me and distracted me by his chatting. He leaned against the refrigerator and talked non-stop about UFOs and the virtues of macrobiotics. I looked at this unwelcome intruder from California with his strange philosophies. In bewilderment I wondered, *Who brought you into this house? Why are you here? Who needs this?*

I forget much of the conversation that evening though we tried to be pleasant externally.

Yet I remember vividly the internal conversation with my thoughts. *Disappointment. Crashing a private party. Personal family plans ruined. Guilt of selfishness.* I went to bed that night, sad and worn out. It was a hard way to learn that trying to serve God on my own terms and time does not bring fulfilment to me or pleasure to Him. I discovered it was not worth setting limits on how and when I would live for Him. From now on I wanted to keep an open heart to bless the people He would send to me.

The apostle Peter had a home of hospitality in which he entertained Jesus and others. He tells us to "offer hospitality to one another without grumbling," (1 Peter 4:9). The J. B. Phillips paraphrase puts it, "Be hospitable to each other without secretly wishing you hadn't got to be!" Giving guests the service of our hands and the polite words of our mouths without love leaves our own spirit drained and dry.

Jesus gave a key to the practice of hospitality when he said, "Anyone who gives you a cup of water in my name because you belong to Christ will certainly not lose his reward" (Mark 9:41). We rob ourselves of the joy of that reward when we lock the inner door of our hearts even though we open the outside door for guests to come in.

The heart of hospitality is love.

VISITING THE LORD

As the youth pastor dropped me off by my house he shocked me with his invitation. "Margaret, there are two women in prison who have recently given their lives to the Lord. They are both murderers. I feel it is time for them to relate to a woman for further discipling. Would you be interested?"

My immediate response was, "I don't even have the language to speak to street people. I've never been in prison. I would be a misfit. I'm like a foreigner and wouldn't understand where they're coming from." Much of the ensuing conversation I have forgotten as I wrestled with an inner voice. *Jesus did say something about what would happen on the Judgment Day. People would be divided into sheep or goats. The sheep were those who visited him when he was sick or in prison. The goats were those who didn't. Perhaps this is my one chance to be sure I would land on the side of the sheep* (Matthew 25:31-40). *In much timidity but daring to try it, I agreed to go.*

In the early 1970s I entered the Lehigh County Jail for the first time. The officers looked intimidating as they checked me in. Guards unlocked doors to let me through and quickly locked them behind me. I thought, *I am lost in this maze of corridors and floor levels. I'm at the mercy of the prison personnel to find my way out again.*

Sitting down to talk to these two inmates guilty of murder I experienced one of the magnificent surprises of my life. All estrangement evaporated in the awareness that we were related in Jesus. Our vocabulary might be different but we had the common language of Christ's love, equally sinners saved by grace. The conversation flowed easily and our hearts quickly bonded in the fellowship that mutual faith in the Lord Jesus gives.

Shortly after this visit I received a phone call from a Christian friend in Allentown who held services for the men in jail. "Would your fellowship group like to be responsible for holding a Sunday service once a month for the women's section of the prison? One Sunday a month has opened up and the chaplain has permitted me to offer it to you." There were one or two others in our fellowship who had felt called to the girls in jail and soon we formed a ministry called *Volunteer Friends.*

We began to feel that once a month was not enough to keep in touch with the women. It was a county jail and therefore, a holding place from which some inmates were moved on to a long-term facility once they were sentenced. Others would be discharged before we had had enough time to ground them in their new-found faith. The Tuesday fellowship which met in our home made this need a project of prayer. *Dear Lord, please make room for us to get in at least two Sundays a month.*

Later we were delighted to hear that some other group had canceled their Sunday slot and the offer was made for us to fill it. *Would it be possible that the Lord would allow us to go in every Sunday for services?* We felt encouraged to exercise greater faith and pray. It was not long before we received the invitation to come in every week — all other groups had withdrawn from their commitments.

Since the early 1970s it has been a special privilege for our teams to lead these Sunday services. The women have listened to our messages with eager interest, their responses evident on their expressive faces. To me their enthusiastic singing sounds sweeter than a church choir. At the end of the meetings they write out their prayer requests knowing that our prayer group will meet weekly and faithfully, taking every request to the Lord. When the guards come in to escort the girls back to their living quarters, they all look for a hug. We embrace them warmly in God's love without thought of the AIDS and other diseases among them.

Over the years the ministry developed into a program of additional Bible studies in the week, handcraft sessions, one-on-one visitations. There were special social events such as a summer picnic, a Christmas party which the wardens and judges were happy to attend. Many of the girls were accompanied by a Volunteer Friend when they went to court and helped to find housing and jobs when they were released.

Sometimes we had to learn hard lessons in a disappointing way. I remember one Christmas message I gave on the theme of the Wise Men's visit to the baby Jesus in Bethlehem. We sat around in a circle and I illustrated my talk with souvenirs brought from Jerusalem. I was so pleased to pass around my little inlaid jewel box containing my treasures of frankincense and myrrh from Israel. I added a gold ring to complete the symbols of the gifts offered by the Wise Men. When I returned home I did not feel so pleased to discover the gold ring was missing! It was naive to trust them with temptation.

Occasionally we offered hospitality to one who was released and needed a place to stay. Eileen came to our home and needed a sweater. I loaned her my good English knit green sweater which I cherished as it was the last gift my Mother gave me. We knew Eileen needed to be supervised constantly and my husband and I needed to go out of town one day. We arranged with our friend Judy to entertain Eileen during our absence. Judy thought a visit to a friend in the hospital would be a good idea. While there Eileen excused herself to go to the washroom. But instead she ran away. And she was wearing my green sweater.

Once again we were disappointed that Eileen would run away and felt compelled to try and find her. Douglas and I drove up to Wilkesbarre, about 40 miles away, without her address but aware that she had relatives in the city. We prayed to be led to the place without any idea what the address was. We were thrilled to locate the house quite quickly. On our arrival Eileen fled for cover afraid that the police were waiting for her once we identified her. *This reminds me of the Proverb which says "The wicked man flees though no man pursues, but the righteous are as bold as a lion"* (Proverbs 28:1).

It took some persuasion to convince her that we came because we loved her and we wanted her to know that we cared for her. She had no idea where the green sweater went but she knew that we came to tell her once again that Jesus loved her. She was learning that in spite of disappointing her Lord by her behavior, He would never disappoint her.

140

Then came the time when our prison ministry leaders, Frank and Catherine Ternigan, joined us for breakfast at a restaurant. An attractive waitress came to serve us and surprised us, "I know you," she said. "I'm one of the girls you visited in prison. My life is back together again and I want to thank you for all your help." Our friends were close to tears, remembering all the years of their leadership in the prison ministry as well as the heartache and prayers. They smiled kindly at her and said, "That's what it's all about. . .a broken, wasted life rescued."

We have often told our friends in prison, "Remember it is God who opened the door to bring you in. He wants you to open the door of your heart to let Him in. When you do, His love and forgiveness will set you free inside. Free from the prison of fear and anger and guilt. He wants you to be truly free when the prison doors open to let you out." Many have responded to that invitation. From the bondage of a cocoon they have emerged to fly, sometimes with fragile wings of faith, into God's open world. Beautiful in God's eyes like a butterfly.

God gives His own unique rewards of joy when we "visit Him in prison."

NEW WHEELS, NEW HEART

I listened with shock to the complaints of the real estate agent's wife as we sat around the table enjoying a ladies' luncheon. "My husband bought me a red sports car," she complained with disdain, "Who needs a *sports* car?" We had spent the last two hours praising the Lord and listening to His Word. Somehow these words pulled our spirits down. I mused in my heart, *How could she be so ungrateful for a new car? I wish a new car was my problem.*

A short time later my husband announced to the family that we were in the market for another car. That was not news to a family who considered we never got out of the market. Car trouble was part of our lifestyle and when we did change cars, it seemed to be an exchange from one worn-out vehicle to another weary one. The brakes, the mufflers, the starter. . .we lived from one fix-up job to another.

"This time we can buy a new car," my husband explained and immediately all six of us perked up with excitement. In no time we were competing with each other to prove the wisdom of our own personal choices. Different sizes, models, colors and features. The discussion was lively as we eagerly tried to sell our own preference, assuring each other of our own superior discernment in taste, mechanical and engineering insights, economic wisdom, automobile knowledge and driving prowess.

One look at my husband at the end of the large table, and I saw his distress. *How is he ever going to satisfy a crowd like us? There is no way that he can please us all.* I spoke to the four children, "We are praying to ask God to give wisdom in the purchase of this new car, but we are all shouting in Dad's ear. There is no way he can hear God's voice when our voices are so loud. Let's just pray and ask God to lead him to the right decision."

My suggestion was well taken and it was given, I thought, with a sincere heart. . .until my husband brought home a silly little Datsun. It lacked all the features of a dream car. It was non-descript cream on the outside and black inside. It was a two-door car for a family of six. It had a shift drive and I had become used to an automatic. *I'll have to get the gift of shift. This car is so small that it will fold up like an accordion on impact. . .and I will probably be the one driving it.*

That night my husband beside me was sleeping the sleep of the just while I tossed and turned like it says in Isaiah 57:20-21, "But the wicked are like the tossing sea, which cannot rest, whose waves cast up mire and mud. 'There is no peace,' says my God, 'for the wicked.'"

The mire and mud I was wallowing in was a mix of disappointment and fear. I felt deeply disappointed that my husband had probably made a bad mistake in his choice. I sensed a fear that this little Datsun was not safe to drive in heavy traffic. I knew that I would not sleep with the turmoil raging inside me.

A little voice within reminded me of God's Word in 1 Thessalonians 5:18. "In everything give thanks for this is the will of God in Christ Jesus concerning you" (KJV). *But, Lord, I don't feel like giving thanks. I know You did not say 'Feel thanks' but 'Give thanks.'* " I could not begin to try to give thanks until I asked forgiveness for the way I felt. *Am I not guilty of the very ingratitude I judged in the real estate agent's wife?* I began to make my confession, *Dear Lord, please forgive me for my wrong attitudes. I feel so ashamed. But you know my heart and I must be honest with how I feel.*

Next I launched into thanksgiving: *Thank you, Lord, that we were able to buy a new car for the very first time, instead of buying someone else's lemon. Thank you, Lord, that my husband had the guts to buy a car he knew would displease his wife.* I don't remember how long the prayer went on, but I do recall marveling how many things there were to give thanks for. *Is this the Holy Spirit helping me to obey God's Word to "give thanks?"* I never finished the prayer. My thanksgivings trailed into sound sleep.

The next morning as I looked at the little Datsun parked in front of our house I was taken by surprise. My heart had shifted from reverse to neutral — looking at it I no longer felt that terrible negative reaction. Nor was I excited by the new car. Instead I was thrilled by the peace within. *God has done heart surgery in the night. He has changed my heart!* The realization brought such joy that I went out to celebrate with a friend, sharing my good news.

About that time there was a Mideast crisis and oil shortage. Cars were lined up for blocks to get their ration of gas. Our little Datsun went for miles and miles on a gallon of gas. The trunk of the car was just the right size to hold the bags of family groceries after shopping each week. The Lord also kept us safe on the road without accident for the life of the car.

We may fall into a mire of shame, too guilty to approach our Lord. Yet He cares enough to approach us.

Like a heavenly surgeon He cuts away the blockage of a distressed heart crying out to Him until it beats again with His peace and joy.

GOD'S SEWING LESSONS

I never liked sewing. The teachers at the missionary boarding school in China tried to teach us some basics, but I was not interested. Our boring hour of weekly mending cast a shadow on the day. I knew the Chinese *amahs* would complete what we did not finish so I dragged out any job. Then came a class in creative sewing. The green-patterned material was supposed to be transformed into a dress, but mine was so bad it had to be converted into a blouse. I soon determined to get through life without sewing!

And life did go on for many years without a sewing problem until one day our oldest son, David, came home from Freedom High School with an extraordinary request. "Mom, I am going to be a Roman soldier in a play and I need you to make me a Roman tunic. The teacher says there are no patterns. You have to make up your own."

What bad timing! We had just moved into our Pastor's house to take care of his four children while they were away. I'd doubled my child-care load and what time did I have to sew? I couldn't really sew anyway, but I was too proud to let my son know that. I expected him to live up to what was required of him. I didn't want him to think that his Mom was a failure.

"Well, David," I began, "I have no time to shop for material so why don't you go to our house and look at what we have there. Choose something and bring it to me." The moment he left I started crying out to God for wisdom.

When David came back with some brown fabric, I faced the moment of truth. *What would the missionaries have done in China when they couldn't buy patterns? What are the basic elements of making a pattern? Obviously paper, pins and scissors. Here we go!* I took the newspaper and made a hole for David's head to go through, took pins and pretended I knew what I was doing attaching pages of the printed paper around his body. I laid the fabric on the large table and had to make a patch to have enough to fit the makeshift pattern and began cutting alongside the pins. Somehow as I began to sew it began to take on a sort of shape and my son, as naive and ignorant as I was on style, was delighted with the result. The only justification for calling it a Roman tunic would be if you put a Roman soldier in it.

I felt it was a major accomplishment and a victory of faith. I had prayed and now I had a testimony — I had actually made a garment that fit the wearer. I mused, *I'm thankful but I don't want any more "sewing testimonies."*

After a reprieve of a few years our youngest son, Peter, came home from junior high school one day with unwelcome news, "Mom, I have the lead part in a play. I'm going to be Voltaire and you have to make my costume in three weeks." When I examined the pattern for it, I saw I would be required to make a lined coat, breeches, a satin blouse with lace ruffs and a button-down brocade vest. I knew the project was out of the range of possibility, so I called the teacher to make my excuses and suggestions.

"Would it be possible to rent a costume? Could we buy one somewhere although we really can't afford it? Could we borrow one of the high school band uniforms as a substitute?" To all my questions the teacher politely replied, "No." Frustrated I exclaimed, "Then I'll have to sew and trust the Lord." To my surprise she responded, "Yes, you will!"

I wasted no further time, instead taking my complaints to the highest authority, *"Lord, you know how busy I am in the fellowship ministry in this house, all the people I am serving in the kingdom for You. I have no time to sew with a deadline like this. Do I have to do it? You'll have to help me. I can't afford the time to make errors and undo and repeat the work. I know I am supposed to do everything 'heartily as to the Lord'* (Colossians 3:23). *Well, I'll try, Lord, but please help!"*

My initial shock at the enormity of the task turned into a pleasant surprise. *"Lord, you're giving me the ability to follow the patterns without mistakes!"* I kept leaning on His help for I had no experience to trust. *The Lord told us that with us it is impossible, but with Him all things are possible* (Matthew 19:26). *I am beginning to believe it.* My faith was riding high until I came to the jacket pocket. The pattern puzzled me and I was still trying to make sense of the instructions when the telephone rang. The caller explained, "I have a problem. Could I come over and talk to you?" *She has a problem? Well, I have a problem!* After a brief pause I knew where my priority stood and answered, "Sure, come over." But I discussed my dilemma with the Lord, *"You know I don't need this interruption. However I know your instructions, 'Seek ye first the kingdom of God and His righteousness and all these things shall be added unto you' (Matthew 6:33, KJV). I am sure people are more important to You than projects."*

When my friend came in the door and looked at all the sewing work on the table she exclaimed, "Margaret, all this sewing. . .I didn't know it was in you!"

"It *isn't*!" I emphatically declared. I went on to tell her about the problem of the pocket and, as one who loved to sew, she got intrigued. She quickly figured out how to do it and the sewing project was finished on time! She had solved my situation but never got to her own!

Sometimes we fail out of fear because we feel the task is beyond us. Our root problem is unbelief. When God knows we want to grow in trust and faith, He may test us. It is then we receive the gold of His grace and give glory to God.

THAT POWERFUL NAME

The day began like any other Monday. The laundry was in process. Three of the four children had left for school and one had stayed home sick with some minor virus problem.

A knock at the door ushered in one surprise after another. Sarah, a friend in the fellowship proclaimed, "The Lord told me to come and help you." I had no sense of need and felt embarrassed by her offer. *Now I have to think of something for her to do or she will feel foolish. What can I dream up?* I tried to be polite and make her welcome, but explained, "I'm not really aware of any need. You could help with the ironing, I suppose. Oh! I nearly forgot. John is home sick with a cold or something. I'm not worried at all about him but you could pray for him if you like." *At least she wouldn't feel so awkward if she had something spiritual to do like praying for someone even when there is no major crisis going on."*

John, 14 years old, lay in bed bored but comfortable when Sarah and I came to pray for him. In five minutes our routine prayer for healing was over. Each of us prayed quietly in our prayer language (the Holy Spirit "gift of tongues") while the other prayed aloud in English. Sarah helped with some ironing and then left.

I heard some strange sounds just before John called out to me, saying, "Mom, I think I have the gift of tongues." We had not encouraged our family to seek the gifts of the Spirit because, in our ignorance, we felt they were too dynamic to be trusted to children. It was only after a long period of cautious inquiry that we had been willing to enter this dimension of Christian experience ourselves. I asked John to pray aloud in his new given language and in my heart, I sensed he had received a genuine spiritual gift. This was immediately confirmed to me by his joy and a new surge of interest in reading the Word of God.

Later that day John called me to his bedside. In fear and distress he blurted out, "I feel I'm dying and going to heaven. Something's choking me." In my shock and inexperience, surely the Lord put the next words in my mouth, "John, if it was the Lord who was telling you that you were going to heaven, you would be so happy." His anxious face visibly relaxed as he thought on this for a moment and asked, "Really?"

"Yes, God doesn't put fear in our hearts. Heaven will be a wonderful place to go to when He calls us there. . .Fear comes from the Devil, and he tells lies." Secretly I called to the Lord in my own crisis, *Dear Lord, where do I go from here? I have no idea how to handle this.*

Quickly words came out of my mouth, "John, we are going to rebuke the enemy in the Name of Jesus and tell him to go away and renounce any hold he may have on you." John agreed and we prayed together one after the other, "Satan we rebuke you in the Name of Jesus Who has all power over you. . ."

"Oh!" sighed John, "it's gone away. . .I don't feel my throat being choked." We marveled at the quick deliverance from fear and an evil manifestation, though I felt sobered by the unexpected emergency. *I'll have to be available to do spiritual warfare at any time of day or night. How can I stay alert at night?* As I noted the anxiety rising within me I remembered the words in Psalm 127:1, "Unless the LORD builds the house, its builders labor in vain. Unless the LORD watches over the city, the watchmen stand guard in vain. In vain you rise early and stay up late. . .for he grants sleep to those he loves."

At bedtime I reminded John, "Today we have seen that the Holy Spirit in you was greater than the power of Satan (1 John 4:4). You also know the power of the Name of Jesus and how to fight back any enemy attack. As you go to sleep let your thoughts meditate on Psalm 23 and God will give you peace and a good night's sleep." In the following days John had no further attacks and we rejoiced in his new enthusiasm to walk with the Lord.

Some years later at a Saturday night fellowship in our home Douglas taught on spiritual warfare. About midnight he was taking off his shoes to get ready for bed when we heard a blood-curdling scream in the neighborhood. *Could those screams be a fire? A murder?* The urgency was alarming. No time to waste.

"Margaret, call the police," Douglas said as he rushed barefoot across the street to investigate. Although we didn't know these neighbors, Douglas dashed into their house safely past two excited German Shepherd dogs without being attacked by them. He found a bewildered babysitter trying to control an 8-year old girl screaming in terror, "I saw it! I saw it!" No words would calm her.

Helpless, Douglas asked if he could pray for her. "Yes" was the quick response. Douglas called out, "Jesus! Help her!" Dramatically the spirit of terror fled, the young girl smiled in relief and quietly went back to bed. Neighbors from many houses around came out on the street to find out what was happening. Four police cars arrived, no longer needed.

In this incident neither a babysitter or a caring neighbor was able to relieve the one distressed. It took a simple prayer in the powerful Name of Jesus.

We will have evil attacks in life. But, Jesus taught us to pray to be delivered from the Evil One. We are also instructed to put on our spiritual armor and fight the enemy with spiritual weapons. When we stand in faith in the Name of Jesus, Satan cannot stand up against Him. He cowers under that powerful Name.

WELCOME SAINTS AND STRANGERS

Some of the beauty and art of hospitality has been brought to my attention by being a generous recipient of this gift. Each home has its own style. We have experienced a diversity of expressions, from casual to formal, from the poor to the rich. Our hearts have been touched not by the menu, but by the motive behind the hospitality offered.

I remember a farmer in Greece riding on his donkey eating his lunch of bread and greasy black olives. The smile on his face is permanently captured in my memory as he opened his hand toward us, to share his meager portion.

Another time in Crete we visited in a home and the hostess brought a tray of two glasses of water and two small plates of sweet preserves. We were puzzled why our hosts were waiting and watching, not joining us. *What is the protocol here? Should we go ahead and eat? Why are we the only ones being served?* A bit embarrassed, we asked them if they were going to participate with us. Their answer went deep into our soul, "These treats are only for guests. If we also ate them we would not have anything to offer in hospitality." We have never forgotten their pure pleasure in giving without receiving.

Another time I had a dream of visiting the community where Mother Basilea Schlink and the Sisters of Mary lived. These are a group of German Lutherans whose devotion to prayer and Christ-like lifestyle have touched thousands of lives. Their hospitality to us at Canaan in Darmstadt, Germany, was unforgettable.

Their daily menus were determined by what the Lord brought in or what they were able to grow on their property. The Sisters looked daily for God's provision and practiced contentment if they had only plums three days in a row. At mealtimes, graciously and formally served, we were fed spiritually as well as physically as one of the Sisters read to us or told us about God's faithfulness to them. Even a box lunch was packed with a Scripture or quote of encouragement printed beautifully. There was a quietness and peace in the midst of much prayer and service.

At the final meeting where about 200 of us met, our son Peter sat, probably the only boy in a room of adults. He knew this weekend was a special gift to Mom and had accepted his lonely role. The Sister in charge of the meeting noticed him, left the room and returned with an illustrated book for Peter to enjoy. It was another expression of kindness and thought extended to the youngest, the least. A teenager could have felt so out of place in this devout community of robed Sisters with radiant faces. For me it had been a taste of heaven. As we drove away, our 14-year-old son sighed with regret, "I never thought I would never want to leave this place."

Another praying "saint" we were privileged to have in our home was Miss Eva McCarthy. She had been one of the survivors of the Titanic tragedy. This godly praying woman so loved the Lord, so exuded a sweet and selfless love, she might have walked out of the pages of Scripture and been an "angel unaware." We sensed an awareness of the presence of Jesus during those few days she lived in our home.

We had many others through the years that challenged our own degree of selfishness or saint-hood. I will introduce a few to you.

We invited one young man we will call Jerry to live with us for awhile. He had been a drug pusher and had given his life to the Lord. He was artistic and we accepted some of his colorful mobiles in lieu of rent as he was short of money. We loved him though he found it hard to come under discipline. I would catch him grabbing a handful of pickles for breakfast which concerned me. He was a diabetic. He could pray fervently and we believed his sincerity in trying to live a new life.

After some weeks we were saddened to notice the telltale signs that he was returning to his old life, ignoring house rules and staying out with old friends on the streets. The fear was confirmed when we received a call from the police, "We have arrested Jerry and he is in jail. Would you be willing to post bail of $1,000?" We knew Jerry needed tough love. "No," we answered, "But we will visit him in the prison." I mused, *Have we lost Jerry forever? Was all our prayer and hospitality in vain — a failure?* Jerry never came back to live with us but some time later we happened to meet him on the street with a gang of guys. To our surprise he broke away from them to embrace us with bear hugs! *At least he heard our message and knows he is loved.*

One evening a pastor called and said, "Our house is full but there is a woman in the Emergency

Department of the hospital being detoxified. The hospital can't admit her. Would you be willing to take her for the night?" We stumbled and staggered up the stairs with this drunken lady and put her to bed. I stayed in the room with her and in the morning she did not have any idea where she was or how she got there. Very quickly I saw her discomfort in trying to fit into our ordered home and though she appreciated our help, she was grateful to leave. I thought some more about the cost of hospitality. *It is right to open our doors to strangers but it takes a special calling and skills to minister to those who need constant supervision and counseling. Perhaps this is not what God has called me to do.*

One morning my husband and all the children had left for college and school and I was alone in the house planning my agenda. As I walked by the washroom on the main floor I noticed the door was closed. When I tried to open it, I couldn't. I was puzzled, then concerned, then alarmed. *Has someone broken into the house? Man or woman? Do they have a weapon? I better find out quickly.*

"Is someone in there?" I asked, trembling in my officious tone.

"Yes" came the weak answer.

"How did you get into the house?"

"Your back door was open and I slept in your basement for the night."

"Well, we need to talk. Meet me at the front door." I was poised to dash out of the house and call for help if the intruder looked dangerous.

The young woman explained that she was running away from a situation at her Bible school and needed a place for the night. "Why didn't you come to the front door and ask us for help?"

157

"I was scared" was her feeble answer. One runaway can disrupt many people's plans. We spent hours contacting friends, family, school authorities, counselors to find out what we should do with this "stray" problem. It was simple to feed her, launder her clothes and meet her immediate needs. I puzzled in prayer thoughts. *What is my duty in hospitality here? She has no money. She's broken relationships. She has to go to work or back to school. Who needs an interruption like this to one's day? My love is wearing a bit thin.*

Our fellowship friends and family joined in praying for wisdom and the next morning a few gathered in our home to confront the stranger. We stood in a circle and words came out of my mouth. "This is God's house and we run a tight ship. We cannot afford to have a Jonah running away from God's assignment living in our home. We have a friend who is willing to drive you back to the school and we have the finances to get you there. You need to ask forgiveness and be reconciled with the authorities there and ask them to give you a second chance. If you are unwilling to do this, we have to let you leave. We cannot let you stay in this house."

To our utter amazement she agreed to go back. The last I heard of her, years later, she was doing well.

Sometimes we think that hospitality is the means of cultivating the love of friends. By welcoming many through an open door, God enlarges our hearts and our capacity to love. On the other hand, by knowing when to gently close the door, we also express God's love of stern mercy in hospitality with discipline.

We are never lonely surrounded by strangers and saints!

WATERING AND BEING WATERED

All the family were packed and ready to go on a six-week vacation to Canada. But it was Sunday so our first stop-over was the morning service at First Presbyterian Church. As usual, we were the last to leave and were parked in front of the Church when we noticed a flat tire.

Why has this happened now? It couldn't have happened at a worse time. How frustrating! There's nothing to do but sit and wait just as we're ready to get going. We thought everyone else had left the Church when our friend Judy appeared with some news. "Pastor Keith is in his office with a problem. A Mexican family of seven people dropped into the Church today. They have no housing, no job and no money. The oldest son has been admitted to West Point, and they all left California to settle nearer to him."

Lord, is this why we are stuck with a flat tire? We have a house with four bedrooms, beds made and food on the shelves and stored in the freezer. Do you want us to offer them our home? Quickly we sensed this was what we were to do. The Pastor was relieved at the immediate solution to his problem and the Mexican family were incredulous to find themselves in a Dutch Colonial home. It never occurred to us to question the character and trust-worthiness of these strangers. Instead, a great joy and excitement came into our hearts at the privilege of giving them a place to live.

Instead of proceeding on our trip we repaired the flat tire and returned to open up our house and give these visitors a tour of the property. We lived in a large home which had a full basement with pantry, workshop and nursery. On the main floor we had a large living room and dining room, a good-sized kitchen, laundry area, powder-room and library. A stately staircase led to the bedrooms and bathroom upstairs with a porch overlooking the back yard and garage. A walk-up attic on the floor above gave ample room for storage. Our guests were overwhelmed in gratitude and disbelief.

However, we also had a temporary problem. We were without running water at the kitchen sink and were obtaining what we needed from houses next door. We apologized for the inconvenience, explaining that Douglas did not have the tools, the time or the expertise to fix the plumbing. To our surprise, the father of this family got right to work and, in no time, our problem was over. Water was flowing out of the faucet.

Before we went on our way we suggested that we join in a circle for prayer in the living-room. We explained to the family that we believed in a God who heard our prayers and would supply our needs. We held hands and talked simply to our Heavenly Father, "Lord, you know this father needs work so we ask that You will help him find a good job. In time they will need to find a place to live. Will you show them where that is and provide for a reasonable place to rent. Thank you for bringing them here. Keep them well and may they enjoy our home just like we do." *They say they are Roman*

Catholics, but do they really know Jesus personally? It seems as if they are so moved, as if this is all new to them — almost beyond belief.

As we left the house to start on our trip some neighbors down the street, also Church members, arrived with a donation of food for these newcomers. "We heard what you've done and we want to help, too, and get in on the blessing!" they said. Later we learned that a number of others from the Church helped in food gifts and friendship. Our house guests regularly attended our Presbyterian Church while we were away, and in time they came to understand what it meant to come to Jesus for salvation and make life commitments to serve Him.

Meanwhile, we were enjoying a restful vacation in Canada, that is until a lightning strike hit a post just 25 feet from our tent. The next morning Douglas was suffering with acute eye pain, possibly caused by the lightning strike. Due to the added complication of very high blood-pressure, the doctor sent him straight to the hospital's emergency room. When he was discharged, we had to return to our home in Pennsylvania, earlier than we had planned.

We called to alert the Church and one of our pastors decided to invite our Mexican family to his home so they would be cared for when our home was no longer available.

We returned to our home to find everything in apple-pie order. The house was clean. The garden never looked better. And the father explained that he now had three job offers and his problem was not *where* to get work but *which* job to choose. Although we had offered the parents our own master bedroom, they had felt unworthy to lie on our bed and chose to sleep on the sofa in the living room. Their gratitude for hospitality given was profound. Best of all, they had found a circle of Christian friends in a Church which welcomed them and introduced them to the best Friend of all, Jesus.

Sometimes our frustrations are God's opportunities; our disappointments are His appointments. We reached out to offer a "cup of cold water" in Christ's Name through the hospitality of our home. Soon our own tap water, turned off for mechanical problems, was fixed and began to flow.

I chuckled to myself thinking how literally this seemed to fulfil the words of Proverbs 11:25 (KJV), "He that watereth shall be watered also himself."

We had the privilege to offer a vacant home to weary travelers who needed to be refreshed. In God's secret of giving and receiving, sowing and reaping, the harvest of joy surpasses the cost of any seeds of sacrifice. Not only was our garden transformed and renewed, but our own souls were refreshed.

BUDGET ITEMS — FAITH AND FUN

One day I asked my husband, "We know so many people struggling in their marriages. And it seems that so many of the problems center around money. Why don't we fight over finances?" His quick retort, "Because we don't have any finances to fight over!"

From early childhood I was taught the principle of spending only what you have and saving what you can. Owe no man anything (Romans 13:8) was one of the foundational policies of the China Inland Mission in which I grew up as a missionary kid.

Our frugality was put to the test when Douglas accepted a four-year teaching position at Yale University many years ago. It was a prestigious job but the annual salary for a new lecturer was just $3,500. I look back on that time as a penny-pinching era in which we learned to do without and learned to live by faith. God's generosity enabled us to keep moving both in the ways of serving Him and in the way of faith.

We lived eight miles from the campus so one of our big needs was transportation. When we were offered an old Ford for $50, we were thrilled to be able to buy our first car without going into debt. God's next provision was a $100 gift from a visiting friend. We felt this gift should be put in savings toward purchase of our next car. But a few weeks later our car was damaged in the raging flood waters of a hurricane. It took almost exactly $100 in repairs to get the car on the road again. *Gone was our careful savings but God had provided for our need.*

One summer in New Haven in 1954 we faced medical expenses from the arrival of our second son, John. We had good friends in our church who owned a successful business and could have hired Douglas. However, we learned that their high respect for academics would not allow them to offer a job to Douglas. In their minds a construction job was beneath his dignity. We prayed and hoped some employer would have mercy in our desperate situation. Then came the day of good news — a summer job for one month serving as a night watchman in an old ladies' nursing home. It was a boring job except when an obese patient fell out of bed and, howling, had to be hauled back in. The best news was that the pay for that month, $100, exactly matched the need for our obstetrical bill.

Part of the problem of budgets is record-keeping. Early in our marriage I felt some friction between us because of our roles and different business styles. I assumed that my husband, like my father, would be the business manager of the house while I took care of the domestic chores. To my chagrin I noticed bills lying around neglected while my dear husband dwelt on the Greek glories of the 5th Century B.C. as he taught students at the University. I was to discover I had married a man with multiple talents and much wisdom. Many a time I have asked him, "How did you know this? How did you know how to do that?" and his standard reply has been, "When you've studied

Greek......" which was supposed to solve the mystery. He quickly resolved our dilemma by delegating the paperwork to me. I delighted in being "financial secretary," a sort of white-collar job in the midst of many menial tasks in the home.

In the early years of child-raising we had a tight budget and had little extra for entertainment. We did go on vacations which we prayed about year by year. We were able to visit our relatives in Canada each year and many times we were invited to cottages or camps as guests or to accept at minimal cost. My weekly "entertainment" was the trip to the grocery store. Douglas came home from the University to give me the pleasure of shopping without children. This outing to me was like playing a game which I could always win. I made the budget, item by item, and calculated the cost to keep within the $15 weekly allowance. In the store I had the fun of making changes, choosing to replace jelly with olives or whatever appealed at the moment. After such juggling and adding the pluses and minuses of each item's cost, the bottom balance was guaranteed. And the game was won.

For years we served refreshments following a fellowship meeting on Saturday nights in our home in Bethlehem, Pennsylvania. We entertained many hundreds of people and each week had enough to serve the folks who came in from all around the area. A bakery generously donated day-old donuts, garbage bags filled with more varieties of donuts than we had ever seen. *We are blessed beyond belief: we are rich in luxuries.*

It took only a few weeks to wonder if we had fallen into the trap of the Israelites who asked God for meat to enhance their manna. God sent quails in abundance and they suffered from their indulgence. We discovered the limitations of our appetites for donuts and the burden of responsibility of huge leftovers. Our Sunday spare time was spent packaging these donuts and driving around to deposit them at other fellowship homes. *This blessing has become a curse. We are wasting our time driving around giving unwanted gifts to others. Too much is too much.* It was a relief to stop the flow. *After all, surely in the Promised Land flowing with milk and honey, enjoyment was proportional.*

Although we maintained a strict control on expenditures most of the time, there would be occasions when I was tempted to break loose. This usually occurred when an opportunity to help in some need came to mind. *Now that we have some savings we can be a little generous.* When I consulted my husband, he would give his standard response, "Margaret, your budget is comprised of slightly absurd economies coupled with wild extravagances!" Most of the time we agreed on the giving. One of our joys has been sharing the savings.

The apostle Paul wrote, "I have learned the secret of being content in any and every situation (Philippians 4:12). We may feel our wants leave us with a longing to be satisfied. And we may discover too much abundance leaves us satiated.

We are rich when we know the joy of contentment.

HEALING FROM ABOVE

One of the blessings which emerged from the Charismatic Movement in the 1960s was a growing awareness of God's power to heal. Douglas and I received the fresh outpouring of God's Spirit in our lives accompanied by the unexpected gift of a prayer language, the "kinds of tongues" referred to in 1 Corinthians 12:10. We also experienced a new love for Jesus and a deepened level of faith to pray for others.

An urgent call came from a stranger in the next town. He introduced himself as John Piccione, saying his eight-year-old daughter, Donna, was critically ill. He explained that as a Roman Catholic he had gone through the church channels for prayers for healing. Now, desperate, he was daring to cross denominational boundaries for help. He truly believed his daughter could and would be healed but she was getting worse. Would my husband come and pray? Douglas immediately responded out of compassion and agreed to go and pray for healing.

"But what is the problem?" he asked.

"She has leukemia and is only expected to live for a few days. The doctors say she is terminally ill but I know she is to be healed."

Douglas later confided his thoughts to me, "Margaret, she has leukemia. I have no faith to pray for that! How did I get into this?" He acknowledged that when he heard the diagnosis his faith level dropped and a fear of failure rose within him. But he had given his word and would keep his commitment to visit and pray.

As soon as Douglas arrived at the home, John's wife, Frances, took him aside. "We are as worried about my husband, John, as we are about Donna. My husband is so convinced that Donna is going to have a death-bed miracle that we are afraid he will go to pieces, even lose his faith, if it doesn't happen." This was hardly a booster to my own husband's wavering faith but, by now, he was moving ahead in obedience to God's call to pray, not with any feeling of triumph or impending success.

Surely it was the gracious leading of the Spirit within that prompted Douglas to speak a word to John before entering Donna's room for prayer. "John, I have no guarantee that God will give us the healing we are asking for. All I know is that He hears our prayers and is loving and kind and good. I know, too, that we never come to Him in prayer without a blessing. Even if He doesn't grant the healing miracle we ask for, He redeems the sorrow He permits. There is always a blessing and that blessing extends to others." John listened, but it seemed he was convinced in his heart that God was about to do a miracle.

Douglas moved into the bedroom and stood beside the sick child. Quietly he anointed her forehead with oil and prayed a simple prayer asking the Lord to touch and heal her. A new confidence and expectancy rose in him. He later told me that he really believed the Lord was going to give a miracle. He sensed something had happened. He returned to me at home with new hope in his heart.

A week later John called Douglas with sad
and disappointing news, "Donna has died." My
husband stood by the phone, stunned into silence.
He puzzled over what it all meant, reflecting, "Why
didn't the Lord answer our prayers? The rug has
been pulled out from under me. Is this the result of
daring to step out and taking the risk of praying for
a miracle in an impossible situation? Was that
prayer all in vain?"

Together we went to the Funeral Home to
offer our condolences to the Picciones. We wondered if perhaps this was the real crisis to which we
would bring some comfort. After all, we knew how
real God's comfort is and can be in the loss of a
child. We could understand the shock and pain but
also the comfort and hope God gives to those who
go to Him in their grief. Yet we both dreaded facing
the devastation of this grieving family.

Just as we anticipated, it was an emotional
scene. Distressed faces and loud wailing brought an
atmosphere of confusion to the place. Out of the
hurting crowd came one with a radiant smile on his
face, hugging us with assurance, comforting us
with his words. It was John, the one for whom we
most feared. "It's all right! It's all right!' he exclaimed, "Donna is with Jesus!"

His response was a miracle we did not
expect nor could we quite believe. What had
brought about the change in John? We could not
attend the actual Mass which followed in their
church but we heard a wonderful report. John and
his family, in front of all those parishioners and
friends, walked up and circled the casket and sang
their praise to Jesus in the familiar hymn, *Amazing
Grace.*

A week later we visited John and Frances
around their kitchen table. Once again we intended

to share the comfort God had given to us in grief. Yet, in this particular school of suffering, it was our turn to sit and listen to God's amazing and tender ways with a young father who was trusting Him with all his heart.

John told how he sat by his daughter's bedside in the hospital still convinced that the God he trusted would intervene with a miracle of healing. Suddenly he became aware of a holy light, the Presence of Jesus Himself, saying to him, "John, it's all right. I'm going to take Donna home with Me." The love and authority of the only One in the universe John could ultimately trust, had visited John with a manifestation of Himself and a word of assurance. John could trust the Lord. And the Lord he loved had spoken. His striving was over and his soul was at peace.

They shared more about Donna's last days which brought more understanding of God's gracious ways. "After you left that day, a week before Donna's death, two things happened. She seemed to improve and we thought she was getting better. The priest dropped by and something strange occurred: Donna spoke in a new language. The priest took the words down and thought it was Hebrew. Can you translate or interpret these words?"

Douglas carefully examined what was written. The Hebrew was a prayer to God. The best translation seemed to be, "I pray to be changed from above."

Sometimes we fervently pray for God's best blessings as we perceive and desire them. At other times, in weakness and confusion, we do not know how to pray. We are told in Romans 8:26-27, ". . .the Spirit helps us in our weakness. We do not know what we ought to pray for, but the Spirit himself intercedes for us with groans that words cannot express. And he who searches our hearts knows the mind of the Spirit, because the Spirit intercedes for the saints in accordance with God's will."

In the mysterious ways of God, Donna was praying to be "changed from above" which we interpreted as meaning a change in heaven. In contrast, loved ones on earth were praying she would be healed while here below. The voice of Jesus brought deep comfort to the heart of a loving father. Yet God had more for these parents mourning the loss of their precious daughter. He turned their mourning into His joy-filled comfort which overflowed in a ministry out of their home to young people who gathered there to learn about Jesus. Paul tells us in Romans 8:28, "And we know that in all things God works for the good of those who love him. . ."

Looking only to Jesus the radiance of His face is reflected a little in ours. Listening to Him we hear Love speak and so we share His comfort with one another. Transformed within from above, we join hands and hearts around our symbol of grief, singing, "AMAZING GRACE!"

95% RIGHT!

When we moved in 1970 to a larger home we sensed the extra space was not just for our own family. We had fellowship groups meeting in our home three times a week: a ladies' Bible study group on Tuesday mornings, a prayer group on Thursdays and an Open House on Saturday nights. One day when friends were helping our son paint his room, he emphatically declared, "This house is the Lord's house, it is for the fellowship not just for our family!" In fact, the owners permitted us to hold a fellowship meeting in the home even before the contract was signed. About 75 people came that night, overflowing into the hall entrance and dining room.

We believed that God did not want us to recruit people to come to the meetings but just to maintain an open front door. Many poured in, friends and strangers, from different churches, universities, nearby towns or even the street. We quickly recognized that all this was God's doing and it was marvelous in our eyes. We praised the Lord, taught His Word, prayed together, shared hospitality, and saw God's blessings of changed lives and answered prayer.

There came a time when I became aware of an undercurrent of criticism and discontent in the Women's Fellowship. *How could that be? This is just an open door of hospitality to hear God's Word.* Perplexed, I said, "I've never heard anything."

"That's because you don't belong to the grapevine — you don't gossip!"

Weeks and months went by and the Lord, in His gracious way, continued to meet with us and bless our weekly meetings. But a shadow, like an invisible weight, brought a heaviness to my heart. *Why should we be robbed of all the joy God is giving us in this ministry? It is His work and He is blessing it. I'm not aware of anything I've done wrong, but I know I'm not perfect. I'll consider I'm 95% right and 5% wrong."* That settled the issue in my mind. I would wait until the critics, 95% wrong, would come under conviction and confess their disloyalty. At that point I would certainly be quick to forgive.

On the Biblical principle of not adding wood to the fire, I decided not to add my gossip so that the strife would die down (Proverbs 26:20). The Lord's Presence was not withdrawn but a slow fire of resentment and anguish began to burn within me. The fire did not spread, but neither was it extinguished inside me.

Next I was reminded of a principle in Matthew 18:15. My silence had not solved the problem, I needed to talk out the issues. We gathered a small group and each described the situation from her point of view. Far from feeling free in the face of honest encounter, the weight around my heart felt heavier than ever. We had hoped that exploring facts and truth would heal the breach. But we were to learn that confrontation without humility and love is not God's way of reconciliation.

While our fellowship continued on and was a source of blessing (we were assisting the underground Church in Russia and reaching out to girls in the Lehigh County Jail), I still felt bound by my own judgments on those whose attitudes and words were wounding me. One evening the leaders of the fellowship groups, husbands and wives, met together for prayer and a Communion service. We stood in a circle and someone opened in prayer. My turn was next and as I began to pray I felt a compulsion to say words I did not want to utter. I finally blurted them out in painful honesty, "And the Lord would have me confess my pride." There was stunned silence. No one, including myself, expected to hear those words out of my mouth. The shock seemed tangible and the wait interminable. Then the next one spoke up, "And the Lord would have me confess. . ." The circle of prayer became a circle of confessions, as each one was prompted by the Holy Spirit.

With sensitive hearts, humbled before each other, we celebrated a deeply moving time of Communion. Not only His Presence was felt but the sweet love of His Spirit flowed among us.

Driving home I reflected on this three-year test of unity in the fellowship. *How I wish I had confessed sooner. I feel as light as a feather—the weight has gone. How quickly God did it!*

Then I heard the Lord speak to me right there in the car. "You think that you were 95% right and 5% wrong, but in My eyes any pride and sin is 100% wrong."

We long for unity and healing of our hurting hearts unaware that God holds the key: "Humble yourselves in the sight of the Lord, and he shall lift you up" (James 4:10, KJV). As we humbly confess and stretch out our hand, not to point a finger, but to embrace in forgiving love, we are healed.

Forgiving and forgiven, we are free!

CONQUERED BUT NOT CRUSHED

Jan, a former art student, was suffering terrible pain in her back. Her mother, June Perryman, became so concerned about her daughter's deteriorating condition that she asked if I would be willing to come pray. I was certainly willing, but Jan wasn't ready to reach out for prayer help from me. She returned to Boston, Massachusetts, and tried to resume her work, but her pain became more intense. She was hospitalized and the fatal diagnosis alarmed us all: cancer of the bones. Now she gave permission to her mother to ask me to come and pray for her.

I remember the awesome responsibility in being asked to fly to Boston to pray for Jan in the hospital. *How am I going to approach her? She is a stranger to me and yet she is in such need.* Lost in my thoughts, I looked out of the window of the plane and saw bright white clouds that stretched as far as eye could see. They were like a heavenly glory covering the dark clouds of the earth below. And as I began my prayer for the Lord's help, these words came to mind:

> *How great is God — how small am I,*
> *Lost, swallowed up in Love's immensity.*
> *God only there, not I.*
> *(Unknown)*

June and I walked into the hospital together, each of us sobered by the terminal crisis facing Jan. I waited in the hall of the Intensive Care Unit, bracing myself for the short five minutes I would have with this young, dying artist. *O Lord, help me. Give me words.* I walked into her room and she lay still with tubes and machines all around her. Perhaps she was as apprehensive as I felt.

Surely when facing ultimates there is nothing more important than getting our lives right with God, I thought. "Jan," I began, "Have you ever given your heart to the Lord Jesus?" In her weakness she seemed to mumble an uncertain answer. I questioned further, "Have you ever openly spoken out a prayer of committing your life to Jesus?" A weak "No" was her response. "Would you be willing to pray that prayer with me now?" I gently led her in a prayer of asking Jesus to forgive her sins and give her His eternal life.

My visitation time was up and I had to leave. I went down to the hospital chapel to pray in preparation for the next and last five-minute visit. *"O Lord, show me what to say, what to do. Somehow minister to Jan in her great need."*

I returned to the hospital room and a question came to my mind. "Jan," I asked, "if you could see Jesus walk in this room right now, what would you ask Him?" Her soft voice answered, "I would ask Him to heal me."

"Yes, Jan, we will pray for healing. Our hearts are so thankful to the Lord Jesus when we know our sins are forgiven and He loves us so much. Our natural response is to want to show our gratitude by following and serving Him. You want to be healed so that you can serve Him too."

"First let me tell you what happened years ago. Jesus was visiting in the home of Mary and

176

Martha. A dinner was given in Jesus' honor and Martha served; it is always a good thing to serve the Lord. Lazarus was sitting at the table with Jesus; it is always a good thing to meet with the Lord. Others were there too. Some came just to see Lazarus since Jesus raised him from the dead; it is a good thing to behold the Lord's miracles. But there was one who gave her most costly gift to the Lord. Mary, with a heart full of love, poured her precious ointment on Jesus' feet and wiped his feet with her hair. Her gift meant the most to Jesus."

I felt prompted in an unprecedented way to make a suggestion to Jan. "I have some oil in my hand and I will pour a little on your hand. Could you in your heart give to Jesus what is most precious to you? Out of your gratitude for Jesus in your holy imagination anoint His feet with this ointment of your love." She agreed and I anointed her hand with oil, asking the Lord to touch her and heal her. My allotted time was over. I gave Jan a quick kiss and left the room to allow her mother a short farewell visit.

I sat waiting in the hall when June came bursting out of her daughter's room exclaiming, "It's a miracle! When I followed you to visit with Jan she was very weak, but I could tell she was beckoning for me to come and stand close to her. Then I knew she wanted me to bring my face closer to hers — and she kissed me! I don't know when she last kissed me. I knew what she was really saying through it, 'Forgive me.'" June was jubilant. Her daughter's countenance was loving and radiated inner warmth and peace. A wound of a broken relationship was healed.

I had known nothing about the strain between mother and daughter and had said nothing about forgiving others. God had spoken into Jan's heart.

So dynamic was the release of spiritual power that Jan was able to walk again down the hospital corridors. It appeared that a physical healing was in process. We were mistaken. There are some things we may never understand this side of heaven. Jan did not recover on earth. She came home to Bethlehem and her mother nursed her for a year while Jan battled cancer and pain.

Not long before her death I stood beside her while the pastor held a brief communion service at her bedside. We reflected on how the Lord waits to be gracious to us, to show us compassion even while we are far from Him, going our own way (Isaiah 30:18). Jan had not received the healing of her body but she knew His healing love—in her relationship to God and her family.

Jesus conquers us to bless us – not to crush us. In response we give to Him what we treasure most — whatever the cost. And the fragrance of that offering fills the house.

BREAKING DOWN WALLS

In the late 1940s, my husband spent a summer doing church planting in the largely Roman Catholic province of Quebec, Canada, a rather hostile territory for a Protestant evangelical. More than once he was greeted with a volley of thrown eggs and tomatoes. Nor were we innocent, for in our hearts and minds we were secretly throwing sticks and stones right back. Part of the hostility came from the political and cultural climate at the time. Also we were raised by families who blamed all that was wrong in the Canadian government on the Catholics. The persecution of Protestant missionaries in South America seemed to confirm our judgments that Catholics were enemies of the faith and of us.

Twenty years later the Pope brought about the beginning of many changes in the Catholic church when the Vatican ruled that Catholic Masses could be conducted in the language of the people rather than Latin. The Bible, previously only read and interpreted by the scholars and hierarchy of the Roman Catholic Church, could now be read by the common people. At the same time there began what was known as the Protestant-Catholic Dialogue in the 1960s.

About that same time I felt called to start a women's Bible Study Fellowship group of our neighbors who lived on Primrose Lane in

Bethlehem, PA. I knocked on every door of our street, half of them Catholics. All were gracious, but not one Catholic ever came to the group. I mused, *Did their priest forbid them? There is a lot of false tradition to be revealed and changed.*

When a Catholic mother with five children moved to the house across from ours we decided to make her family a fellowship group prayer-project. Her husband was in Vietnam and she appeared grateful that we would pray for his protection and safe return though she never once joined our prayer fellowship group. The day he arrived home our entire group of Protestants expressed our joy and welcome by standing outside our door and singing, "Praise God from Whom all blessings flow." *This way we can show we cared and give glory to the God Who cared for him.*

In the climate of a slow thaw, relationships through dialogue between the church leaders of both Catholics and Protestants began to warm up. An experiment of an inter-faith community worship service was launched. It was a well-intended but feeble attempt. Each group did not know the hymns and songs of the other and the weak singing failed to lift our spirits. *This just shows how big the gap between us is. We can't even sing in praise together properly. But it's a beginning.*

In the late 1960s through the 1970s we experienced unprecedented blessings in our home and community fellowship groups. Through what is known as the Charismatic Movement, God poured out His Spirit on those to whom He graciously gave a thirst for more of Him. People were saved and received gifts of the Holy Spirit, such as speaking in other languages, healing and deliverance from demonic influences. In our home we now had not only the women's fellowship group on Tuesdays, but a prayer group on Thursdays and an Open House on Saturday nights. Without any publicity or promotion people began to pour into our home. Most amazing was to see Roman Catholics, Russian Orthodox, Greek Orthodox and many mainline Protestant denominations represented. *This is awesome. This is God's work — something quite beyond our influence or control.*

We quietly observed the way the Holy Spirit gently does His work. As we taught God's Word, He faithfully revealed the truths to those who listened. We did not need to argue our theological differences and engage in controversies. Rather, we marveled at the childlike openness of those who lapped up the "milk of the Word" and soon, taught by the Holy Spirit, began sharing insights God was giving them. By exercising their faith these new Catholic and Orthodox Christians developed muscle and meat and fed some of us older Protestant Christians.

At one community fellowship meeting there was a ministry time in which my husband spoke out in a prophetic way as he laid hands on strangers. Suddenly there was an eruption of joy among these people. Who were they? Roman Catholic nuns and priests! Douglas, through the gift of prophecy, had confirmed their calling to South America where they became leaders in the renewal there.

The Allentown Catholic priest, a leader in his diocese, invited Douglas and myself to be two of 20 Protestant guests to attend the Roman Catholic Charismatic Convention in Atlantic City, New Jersey. We were given beautiful ocean-view accommodations and had front seats in the huge auditorium seating 16,000 people. As we looked around the hall decorated with banners, I whispered to Douglas, "Look, not one of these banners would be out of place in a Protestant Church: "Jesus is Lord" and "Praise the Lord" and many others.

We walked along the boardwalk one evening and passed thousands of conferees parading in the opposite direction. Like waves of praise to God we heard one group singing familiar songs such as, "Seek ye first the kingdom of God," and another, "Amazing Grace," and another group singing, "Turn your eyes upon Jesus" and on and on. We were returning to our hotel room, but we could have comfortably joined that massive parade which spanned the boardwalk.

We stopped by one of the oceanfront places to have an ice cream. We noticed a couple sitting at the counter for their snack. By the name tags they were wearing we could tell they were attending the same conference so we invited them to join us at our booth. We were deeply moved to discover they were French Canadians from a town in Quebec not far from where my husband had served 30 years before. *Lord, what changes You have brought about. Here we are in sweet fellowship with these who years ago, as Roman Catholics, we would have considered enemies of the faith. Thank you for giving us this surprise and joy.*

We were so moved by all the hospitality and kindness extended to us that our Protestant group wrote a heartfelt letter of thanks to the leadership who had invited us. This was read aloud to the whole audience in the evening meeting. Next, we could hardly believe our ears. Father Bertolucci, the emcee of the meeting, called out, "Would all Protestants in this gathering please stand up?" Our two front rows stood up and there was a scattering of others around the hall. "Now," he went on, "I do not want one Protestant to stand alone. I want a Catholic to go to each Protestant and, eyeball to eyeball, confess the hostility you have felt towards each other." *Without any warning? Forced to confess?*

A young man came toward me to carry out the ritual of apology. My thoughts raced as he approached me, *Oh, young man, I honor your obedience but you are too young to know and understand the historic persecutions of the past.* We dutifully acted out an attempt of confession and reconciliation.

Then I saw a middle-aged nun, perhaps an official of a convent, standing in front of me. Without words we fell into each other's arms, deeply sobbing, holding one another in a long embrace. The ways of God are still a mystery to me. God's Spirit stirred something deep in the hearts of two strangers and hidden wounds of hostility in the depths of our soul were healed. Without words His forgiving, loving Spirit flowed between us and broke down the painful walls of partition.

There was a great release of joy and praise that followed this time of reconciliation. Not only our spirits soared but, set free in our hearts, we danced for joy in the aisles, praising the Lord together. The joy of repentance.

When there are no dividing walls between us, Peace and Praise dance together.

TENTING AND TRUSTING

One spring day in 1976, I was throwing out the trash when I noticed a newspaper article about our friend Stacey Woods, founder of InterVarsity Christian Fellowship in North America. Stacey had started this outreach to high schools and universities in the 1930s, and Douglas was among the first participants. Later on Stacey moved to Lausanne, Switzerland, as Director of the International Fellowship of Evangelical Students in Europe.

Stacey also pastored an English-speaking congregation in Lausanne, and the article in my hand was an appeal for someone to replace him for two Sundays during the latter part of July. *Surely Stacey would have many contacts whom he could invite to preach for him. Is he that desperate that he needs to advertise?* It so happened Douglas had been invited to be a visiting professor at the American School of Classical Studies in Athens in September. Earlier that month he was to speak at a conference in Schloss Mittersill, Austria. *Should he offer to be of help to Stacey? It would mean that we had no plans for August, of course. We couldn't afford to tour in Europe for a month. But Douglas could preach for two Sundays.*

When Stacey learned that my husband was available he gratefully accepted his offer. We were promised an apartment for the two weeks in Lausanne, but the month of August was still a blank on our calendar. We decided to trust God to fill it, and set to work packing and planning for this extended trip. The details seemed endless. We needed to plan home-schooling for 14-year-old Peter who would be taken out of school to travel with us. We needed to rent our home, take care of the cat, pack clothes for all seasons, arrange for the car, hand over leadership for the ministries that met in our home. Then there was endless red tape: forms to fill out, visas, passports, tickets, correspondence over schedules and housing in Athens with a maid, arrangements to buy a Fiat in Italy, finances, address changes, keys. . .*How can I possibly keep track of everything? The list gets longer and longer. I'm sure we will miss some detail and find ourselves in a major crisis.*

The pressure started to overwhelm me, especially the responsibility of not making a mistake. As I lay on my bed, exhausted from the emotional overload, the Lord spoke to me, *My love and my power are so great that I can forgive all your sins so that you can have eternal security.* I responded quickly with a "Yes, Lord." I fully believed in the forgiveness of sins and the gift of eternal life. Then I heard Him speak again. *My love and my power are so great that I can redeem all your mistakes so that you can have earthly security.* That was what I needed to hear. I needed security in the "here" as well as the "hereafter."

There was still another issue that loomed large in my mind. Where were we going to live during August? We were on a tight budget and costs in Europe were high. Douglas was far more concerned about academic challenges than with our housing crisis. When I reminded him that we could not afford hotels for a month, he quickly solved the problem, "We can tent!"

My anxiety sky-rocketed at the very thought of tenting. I had reason for my fear. A few months before we had taken a friend's offer to tent by a private pond. Late one night we were rousted from our sleep by intruders hurling M-80 firecrackers. "You have ten seconds to come out of that tent or we'll shoot!" they demanded. Douglas scurried out in his pajamas and convinced the men that we weren't trespassing. Both fled the scene after Douglas stood up to them, and they were later picked up by the police.

So when my husband said we could tent during August, a flood of memories came back to me. Practical problems also piled up in my thoughts. *How could I pack all that gear for tenting? How could I shop in Europe for food when I don't speak the languages? What are we going to do?* I carried these anxieties for weeks and attempted to carry the cares to the Lord in prayer as well. When it was time to depart on our journey we still had no resolution in sight.

We landed in Europe during a prolonged drought. At one train stop we formed a circle on the platform with strangers we met to pray for rain. The newspapers were declaring it was the worst drought in a century and the forecast was no rain for two more months. As we rode on in the train a patter of raindrops hit the window and all the passengers shouted for joy. At the next stop they danced on the platform with excitement.

By the time we arrived in Lausanne, it was pouring rain. *God has done a miracle! He has opened the windows of heaven and is pouring down a blessing. What an extraordinary answer to prayer!*

The young couple who met us at the train station took us to the apartment where we were to stay for two weeks. They graciously welcomed us warmly over a hot drink as we talked for a few minutes.

We sat in unbelief at the next words we heard. "Our missionary parents, who live in this apartment, are on furlough on the mainland of the United States. They are going to be gone longer than they had planned. They will not be returning for six weeks. Would you like to stay here during August, or, at least make this your headquarters if you wish to travel around?"

O Lord, forgive my unbelief. Why did I worry so much? Why did I doubt your love to provide a place for us? Now I am overwhelmed by your kindness. And I can hardly believe it!

We gratefully accepted, and later I noticed a little picture text on the buffet in the dining area. It was a paraphrase of Zephaniah 3:17. To us it was a message from heaven:

HE IS SILENTLY PLANNING FOR YOU IN LOVE

God's power and love is so great that He can open the windows of heaven to pour down the blessing of rain to a continent in drought. And His power and love is so great that He can open a door for one family in need of a place to live.

NEW HORIZONS

During our time in Lausanne, Switzerland, we met a couple of staff from the Youth With A Mission (YWAM) training center at the church where Douglas was preaching. They invited us to the chalet where schools were in progress at YWAM's headquarters. We were impressed by the variety of speakers and staff, their warm hospitality and welcome.

Douglas was invited to speak at YWAM's weekly meeting. That night a young man visiting from France who had a history of drug abuse dedicated his life to the Lord. We sensed God's presence and blessing in that place. Another time we were surprised by a private donation presented to us anonymously. *What kind of missionary group is this? They are not only living on faith for their own finances but sharing what they have with outside visitors!*

We observed the cross-cultural, international, inter-denominational harmony in their lifestyle. The vision of the mission to support all churches by encouraging staff to link up with many different ones was exemplary. This served as a model for our own home fellowship groups in which we saw many hundreds participating from a wide variety of church backgrounds.

Among the participants of our home fellowship back in Pennsylvania was a young couple,

Dennis and Jo Fahringer. They asked for prayer and counsel about their missionary future. When they were exploring the possibility of joining Youth With A Mission, we shared our experience and encouraged them in that direction. For eight years they served in YWAM in Heidebeek, Holland.

Now Douglas and I were facing a crossroads. The time had come, after four years of teaching at Yale and thirty years at Lehigh University, to consider what we would do in our retirement years. Before our marriage we had each applied separately to be missionaries overseas, but the door had been closed to both of us.

Douglas's father, Charles Feaver, took early retirement from his position as vice-president of Frigidaire, General Motors. He then served fifteen years as President of the Shantyman's Christian Association in Canada. He described this period of ministering to miners, lumbermen, fishermen, lighthouse keepers and others in lonely places, as the best years of his life. This set a dream in his son's heart who always looked on his Dad as a model of Christian service and leadership.

One day in 1984 we received a letter from Loren Cunningham inviting us to come to a Founders' Fellowship Week being sponsored by Youth With A Mission in Kailua-Kona, Hawaii. We were to be guests while on the island but needed to pay our own airfare. The invitation came in January just a few weeks before the new semester started in February at Lehigh University. *How ridiculous to go all the way from the East Coast to Hawaii for one short week! Our vacations are always longer than that. How embarrassing to ask permission from the Dean for time off to go to Hawaii at the start of a new semester! How could we possibly justify a request like that at this late date?*

It was also time for our youngest son, Peter, to return to Harvard University after the Christmas holidays. As we were driving him to Cambridge, Massachusetts, we got talking about our dilemma. "But Peter, the invitation is from Loren Cunningham, President of Youth With A Mission, to be their guests for a week in February. Of course, the idea is absurd. The timing is all wrong. It's so awkward to know how to answer Loren. We feel like fools to ask the Dean for a week off in February. But it's only courtesy to respond to this invitation. How can we be honest and say "No" with integrity if we haven't even asked?"

In a determined, prophetic voice Peter's immediate response startled us, "You should pursue it with all diligence!" *Is that our son speaking? He sounds as if he has the authority of a prophet!*

So Douglas mustered his nerve and raised the subject to his colleagues at the University. To his surprise they not only agreed to the proposal but were enthusiastic. They sat down immediately to work out a schedule to cover his classes to make the trip possible. When he came home to report this unexpected turn of events we asked another question. *Is this really you, God? You know that we don't spend that amount of money for a vacation and certainly not for one week only. What about the cost of the airfare?*

With the reluctance of disbelief we dragged ourselves to the travel agent where we found another surprise. "United Airlines has a Super Special airfare going to Hawaii for just the period of time you are looking at. It is $10 less than the round trip fare to Chicago!" *That is such a bargain that we can't afford to miss it!* We felt we were being moved along a strange, new path. We still needed time to think and pray about it. Our travel agent did not need the time. He told us the next day that he had made reservations for us because he knew we should take this incredible opportunity!

So we started a new adventure which began in Hawaii at the Founders' Fellowship Week. The hospitality was extraordinary and the days filled with challenging and inspiring messages. It was a mind-boggling exposure to global missions beyond anything we had experienced before.We learned that our invitation had come through a contact between Loren Cunningham and Dennis and Jo Fahringer. In a meeting in Holland Loren mentioned that he had leaders to pioneer six out of the seven colleges for the new University, then called Pacific and Asia Christian University. He needed someone for the College of Humanities and International Studies, but was unable to find anyone within the mission for this task. Dennis suggested Douglas to Loren. It was like a swinging door — Douglas had recommended YWAM to Dennis and eight years later Dennis recommended Douglas to YWAM.

One morning at the Kona Lagoon where we were staying as guests during our Founders' Fellowship Week, I was looking on the ocean and marveling at the whirl of recent events. Douglas had been invited to write a curriculum for the new College of Humanities and International Studies. It would require taking a six- month sabbatical in order to do this. Here I was looking out on the Pacific, the ocean I had crossed from China to America as a teenager over forty years before. *Is this another major change in our life together? Is this a missionary call? Where is it going to lead?*

The Lord spoke to me through Psalm 32:8-9. "I will instruct you and teach you in the way you should go; I will counsel you and watch over you. Do not be like the horse or the mule which have no understanding but must be controlled by bit and bridle or they will not come to you."

I felt a sense of security as I meditated on God's promise to guide and counsel and watch over us. But it was the next section which caught my attention. I reflected and asked the Lord what He was saying to me? My lofty spiritual thoughts became rather mundane when I realized I was the mule resisting the new adventures God planned for us. And I quickly surmised that Douglas was the horse, eager and chafing at the bit to go!

Though we may have had no understanding of the road ahead, God had drawn the map for us. He promised not only to instruct us, but also to go with us.

WASTING WORDS

We never dreamed of the adventures awaiting us after the lecture phase of our Crossroads Discipleship Training School in 1985. We had been reluctant to go to such a school at all, feeling we were seasoned quite well in age and experience. But the founder and the Provost of the Pacific and Asia University (later called University of the Nations) had made it clear that, like everyone else, we could only enter Youth With A Mission through one narrow door—attending the Discipleship Training School. We pocketed our pride and decided the privilege of setting the curriculum for the College of Humanities and International Studies was worth the humility of going back to school to learn the basics of Christianity.

Before the three months were over, however, we could not contain our gratitude for the blessing of sitting at the feet of many godly and gifted speakers. The truths they taught were not new to us, but we ate them up like fresh-baked bread. Each speaker's portion was uniquely flavored by the specific insights and wisdom of his or her own walk with the Lord. We yearned that each Christian sitting in a church pew in America could have the privilege of sitting at these feasts and learning more of the ways of God.

Going on the outreach following this school had not been in our plans but apparently God had planned it for us. He changed our minds and put the money in our hands through the generous support of our church. Douglas postponed the writing of the College curriculum so that we could join our team of 40 students on a mission tour of the Philippines, Hong Kong, the People's Republic of China and Korea.

As we formed a prayer circle before departure from the Keahole-Kona airport, Pastor Ed Scratch spoke to us. "You are like a wheel with 40 spokes," he said, "and Jesus Christ is the hub at the center. As long as you all move in unity you will go places with God's blessing. Remember that each 'spoke' has its own individual place and function. Your personal experiences and effectiveness will differ from country to country. Do not compare yourselves with one another."

We left on our missionary journey with great excitement, high expectations and a degree of trepidation. *Am I really fit to be evangelizing the heathen in foreign lands? I've never collared and converted people on the streets. What are we getting ourselves into?*

Every stop brought new adventures in faith. In the Philippines my escort was a new convert, a former murderer who called me "Mom" and followed me through the streets of the barrio to protect me from possible dangers. We celebrated Easter with a Philippines mountain tribe. Our congregation combined nursing mothers, wandering chickens and cats, and a man dressed in his finery with a formal jacket and a G-string. The music was provided by a pipe organ put together by Douglas from scraps of copper piping. Up in Baguio we helped in a hospital teaching basic nursing care. The authorities were so grateful that they offered to give us an appreciation reception when it was time to leave.

In Hong Kong we relieved the overloaded YWAM staff. One of my assignments was a culinary challenge to make scrambled eggs on one occasion and cake on another for 200 people. It was a scary venture, never having cooked for large numbers, but we made it. We talked with Filipinos in the park, helped with the feeding of street people and prayed nearby as others did street evangelism.

In Shanghai we visited the park and tried to make conversation with some eager to practice their English. When the response was, "I have dog. You have dog?" I decided I had failed miserably as an evangelist. We were able to smuggle some Bibles to a contact who would deliver them to others in need. We also made a memorable trip to Chefoo, the port town where I went to school as a child.

Later we flew to Korea where we stayed at a summer camp. Our team also had opportunities to do street evangelism and conduct meetings in churches.

Returning to our Presbyterian Church in Bethlehem, Pennsylvania, we were bursting with enthusiasm to give our reports on the outreach. We were given five minutes between us in two morning services and warned to observe the time limits due to a new schedule of squeezing in three services on Sunday morning.

Both of us wrote out our highlights and rehearsed them carefully. We wanted to pack our allotted 150 seconds with headlines of many of our mission adventures. Douglas spoke first and caught the eye of a professor friend from Lehigh University. He couldn't resist departing from the script in a moment of enthusiasm. I followed with my part of our story. The congregation broke out in applause and we felt gratified that they had caught our enthusiasm until, between services, our Missions Pastor somberly asked us, "Did you realize that you spoke for 15 minutes and the Senior Pastor had to cut out the third point of his sermon?" Utterly deflated and incredulous we promised to cut short our report in the next service. Again the response of the congregation was a heart-warming applause but we knew we had disappointed the Missions Pastor and overspent our ration of time.With chagrin we took tapes of both services back to our apartment and calculated the exact amount of overtime we had stolen. Our guilty consciences demanded an abject apology. Douglas wrote:

Dear Pastor:

Margaret and I replayed the tapes made of our talks during the second and third sessions of morning worship yesterday, and confirmed the AWFUL TRUTH. We had gone over our allotted time — Margaret by a minute and three quarters, but me (I am truly ashamed to say) by over five minutes. Our total time was a little over 12 minutes! Even the second time we only succeeded in cutting it down to eight minutes.

Under normal circumstances this would be inexcusable, but under the unusual time pressures everyone is working under, the crime is compounded. Then to add insult to injury, you had to cut your own sermon!

I realize that mere words are scarcely an adequate apology, but I do not know how else to express my deep chagrin at what must have come across as very thoughtless and selfish behavior.

It is no excuse to say that I just got carried away from my notes and what I had written out to take the prescribed 2 1/2 minutes. I can only hope that the Lord can somehow redeem this blunder and that, in the meantime, you will be able to find the grace to forgive us.

With Christian love,
Douglas

While Douglas was writing, I was reading my Bible in an attempt to get some comfort from the Scriptures. Instead of comfort, the counsel of God's Word seemed to cap our humbling:

"Guard your steps when you go to the house of God. Go near to listen rather than to offer the sacrifice of fools, who do not know that they do wrong. Do not be quick with your mouth, do not be hasty in your heart to utter anything before God. God is in heaven and you are on earth, so let your words be few" (Ecclesiastes 5:1-2).

God's words are always more precious than gold. But there may be times when we need to learn that, for us, silence is golden.

STORING RICHES

From my earliest childhood I was taught to treasure the Bible and store passages of it in my memory. Douglas and I tried to pass on that value as a lifestyle to our children. As we gathered around the table for family prayer time, we started with a child's version of illustrated Bible stories. As the children grew older we used a study guide called Scripture Union which suggested daily portions to read with accompanying notes. At bedtime we went through various memorization schemes such as going through the alphabet and learning a verse with its reference beginning with A, B, C and so on. On vacations were worked on memorizing entire chapters.

In their teenaged years, our children sometimes lacked the means to buy birthday gifts so I suggested my preference for a "spiritual" gift, a Scripture verse recited for the occasion. I remember with amusement one of my first birthday gifts:

> Remove far from me vanity and lies:
> give me neither poverty nor riches;
> feed me with food convenient for me
> Proverbs 30:8 (KJV)

I wasn't sure what was the motive or the birthday message behind that gift! More significant, the tradition of giving gifts of Scripture was begun.

The importance of learning and memorizing Scripture was poignantly illustrated the summer we moved from New Haven to Bethlehem in 1956. We heard of a flash flood which burst on a Christian camp at night in a Pennsylvania valley. A torrent of water swept many to their deaths. One mother was able to grasp the limb of a tree but was unable to save her children. In the watery nightmare she clung to the branch and in her heart she took hold of the comfort of God's Word. She spent that terrifying night recalling the Scriptures which she had memorized. God's Word kept her steady and sane in that dreadful storm of destruction and grief.

I remember my mother, Gertrude Seaman, telling me how she survived when, at the outset of World War II, she and my father were taken captive by the Japanese and forced into a concentration camp in Shantung, China. I had left China at the age of 17 to study in Canada, but for three and a half years of their internment, we could not communicate. They longed to know what and how I was doing. They knew how naive and vulnerable I would be after living all my school life in a missionary compound. How was I adjusting to civilization in Canada during World War II?

She told me many years later that God gave her a comfort promise from Scripture which kept her sanity in those anguishing years of our forced, silent separation: "I know whom I have believed, and am persuaded that he is able to keep that which I have committed unto him against that day (2 Timothy 1:12, KJV).

"That was what kept my sanity during that ordeal," my mother told me.

During our Crossroads Discipleship Training School outreach in the Philippines, we visited a tribal village up the mountain from Baguio. A worried mother sat by her house in despair. She told us she was anxious about her daughter who had been lured into the city with the promise of a job. She had not heard from her daughter for several weeks and feared she might have been trapped by wicked men who were known to ship these innocent girls elsewhere as prostitutes.

I looked in compassion on this distraught mother. *O Lord, what can I say to comfort her? She has a viable reason to be in fear and grief.* In that moment the memory of my own mother flashed in my mind. With a translator I told my story and how my mother was given the faith and courage to trust her daughter to God. Like a desperate soul hanging on to a lifeline, she listened to Paul's words of faith to Timothy, "He is able to keep that which I commit to Him. . ."

She nodded her head in assent as a smile slowly spread across her face. *O Lord, it was painful to go through all those years of silent separation but I can't describe the deep joy of bringing comfort from Your Word to this anguished mother.*

God's truths are like treasures which we discover by digging in His Word. When stored in our minds and memories, we can draw them out to help us through the experiences of life. In our fires of testing they become refined gold — riches that yield pure joy to give away.

EXODUS FROM THE RED
SEA — PART 1

I had a dream — a deep longing. It was not for houses, cars and clothes. Not for position, fame and riches. It was a yearning to return to the place in China where I grew up as a child. It had been over 40 years since I graduated from the missionary boarding school in Chefoo (now called Yentai) in the northeast coast of Shandong. In the early years of the 1940s, I felt cut off due to the strict censorship and eventual break in mail communications during World War II. When internees were released from the Japanese concentration camps after the war families were reunited. But a bamboo curtain of communism came down and once again China was like a closed country.

In the early 1980s it became possible to travel to China, usually with a team of people under the supervision of a tour guide. The alumni association of our Chefoo school organized some deluxe tours. I would look at the attractive brochure and think to myself, *That is so extravagant and the time in Chefoo itself so short. I would love for the opportunity to be part of a ministry trip, a gift from the Lord.* That is just what the Lord gave to me!

While attending the Crossroads Discipleship Training School (CDTS) at YWAM's Pacific & Asia Christian University (now University of the Nations), we knew our class would be going on a two-month outreach in Asia. We learned later that our class would be the first to visit mainland China. Our school leader, Peter Jordan, had been a student in the same school as I in China and shared our excitement about returning to that land. Our class divided up into four teams and Douglas and I chose to go on the ship to Shanghai. As plans were being formulated we felt we should not pressure Peter but rather raise the possibility of the two of us taking a side-trip from Shanghai to Yentai. We could hardly believe our ears when Peter said, "Go for it!"

In our bags we were concealing Bibles and Christian books and pamphlets to pass on to Christian contacts in Shanghai. One of our party of YWAMers was caught reading <u>God's Smuggler to China</u> right out on the open deck! Shocked, our escort from Hong Kong grabbed the book and threw it overboard! Douglas had put an electrical gadget on top of his Bibles and clothes in his suitcase. When the customs' officer asked if he had anything to declare, Douglas declared this gadget. Much to my chagrin he quickly added, "Would you like to see it?" I thought, *How stupid! Now we will be caught and arrested. Oh Douglas! Why didn't you close your mouth instead of offering to open your case?* But the officer's words were a greater surprise, "That is not necessary. You are a righteous man." So we passed through the gate safely.

On the weekend Douglas and I left the team to go to Yentai on a World War II vintage Russian plane. We wondered if we would survive the trip in this noisy relic. When the nose of the plane angled upwards, our baggage slid backwards down the aisle and then returned to us when the plane pointed downwards. But thankfully, we arrived safely and spent four wonderful days exploring the place of my school days.

The actual compound had been converted into a communist Chinese naval base. We could glance at some of the buildings over the wall, but we yearned for a closer look. One time we went to the main gate and gestured to the sailor-guard who appeared to nod permission for us to enter. It was pouring rain and we were disguised by our rain-coats and possibly he had not noticed our Caucasian faces. As we stepped into this base we noticed people walking around not noticing us. *Do we really have permission to be here? We are carrying Bibles. Are we invisible to these people?* I quickly pointed out some of the significant buildings and noticed some of the changes in the roads and decided as quickly to get out. We reasoned, *We are foreigners after all. We are supposed to be traveling as tourists but if we are trespassing on military property we could get not only ourselves but also the young guard at the gate in trouble.*

As I retraced my childhood steps, memories flashed back almost everywhere — the crowded streets, the colorful sights of the marketplace, and even the raw sewage smells of the *Eau de Cologne* valley we passed through on our weekly trek to church, holding our noses as we marched along in pairs. It was sad to see our former Union Church boarded up. Yet there was a church alive in the town and we attended a service there. We were the only foreigners in that packed church and we felt we were being watched by a government agent.

Our hearts were stirred by the enthusiasm of the song leader teaching the people to memorize the hymn, *What A Friend We Have In Jesus*. This was a hymn my husband had sung in French in Quebec, in Greek in Athens, and now he was learning it in

Chinese. The author of this hymn lived only a few miles away from where Douglas grew up in Canada. He wrote the now-familiar words originally as a poem and sent it to comfort his mother while she was sharing his grief at losing his fiancee who was drowned the night before their wedding.

After the service the elderly Chinese showed their welcome by their smiling faces and stretched out hands towards us. But before we knew it, someone grabbed our arms and whisked us upstairs to a room where we were served tea.

Later on I stood at the local beach and reflected on all my memories of that place — swims and picnics, boating races, Children's Special Service Missions with lanterns and competitions of sculpting Scripture verses in the sand. Over the wall was the Memorial Hall where I had nervously given my first "sermon" of five minutes before the audience of my peers and missionary teachers and parents. *What an ordeal that had been. How much prayer went into it! A triumph in spite of timidity. That was my first test. Back then I never dreamed how much public speaking I would be doing.*

Fishermen were mending their nets on the beach and I thought back to the day I was baptized there as a teenager. God had revealed Himself to me in a deep way so that I entered into a new awareness of the power of His Presence through the Holy Spirit. I turned around and looked on the hills still standing as God the Creator had formed them. I looked across the sea and there was the Lighthouse on our favorite island still beaming a warning to ships that pass by. That light, still blinking its code, was like an unbroken link to my childhood passed in this place.

I stood on the beach and wept. Over forty years had passed. Others had passed on too. Catastrophic changes. Wars. Separations. Concentration camp. Death. But the God of the hills had not changed. The Holy Spirit is still present with us. And Jesus, the Light of the World, still shines the same yesterday, today and forever.

EXODUS FROM THE RED SEA — PART 2

It was time to leave Yentai (Chefoo) with its treasured memories and to reconnect with our Crossroads outreach team in Hong Kong when we found ourselves in a crisis of bad weather. Planes were grounded and ships were kept anchored. Our only hope was to leave the city by train. We felt helpless. Throughout our four days we had not seen any other foreigners on the streets, in the stores and restaurants and only one or two in the hotel. We could not negotiate a ticket change on our own. Our attempts to locate the China Travel Service agent in town had been futile.

We were eating breakfast the day before we were to leave when a gentleman came to our table and introduced himself in English. To our intense relief we found ourselves talking to the very person we had been looking for. Very kindly he did what we could not have done for ourselves. He went to the airport, canceled our plane tickets and got a cash refund. Then he went to the train station, purchased tickets and made reservations for us. When he asked how we had enjoyed our visit I expressed the frustration for other alumni who visited only seeing our school compound from outside the wall.

"We are former students of this place returning to the memories of our childhood and have no interest in the political agendas or government secrets. All we long to see is the place we came to love while at school. Would it be possible for you to procure permission for us to see the buildings? We have come after many years and from long distances to see this place so special to us." To my surprise the agent answered sympathetically, "Yes, I have watched some of your groups visiting with tears down their faces. We will need to ask the authorities."

Some years later I was glad to hear that the Communist government had indeed granted limited access for alumni of the school to enter the base and view the buildings from the outside.

Very early on Monday morning we left for the train station, pushing our way farther and farther past many cars until we reached the "Shanghai" car. When we offered our ticket to the young woman agent she clearly found a problem. *Are we not going to get on this train after all this*?

From the deep recesses of my mind came forth words I had forgotten I ever knew, "Bu shi jiantien?" In other words, "Is it not for today?" Our anxious faces and longing looks must have touched a core of kindness in the officials. On and off the train they went discussing our dilemma and, at last, gestured for us to get on. We were given a compartment to ourselves for the 26 hours of our ride to Shanghai.

We were very grateful for a place to lie down though less appreciative of the propaganda music over the loudspeaker, including Stephen Foster music played on Chinese musical instruments, repeated every hour from 6 a.m. to midnight. Douglas tried to stop the sound by stuffing a pillow against the speaker, but we couldn't escape the incessant barrage to our ears.

A passenger stopped by our compartment wanting to talk. In a faltering way Douglas attempted to get into a significant conversation with him. We were carrying some Christian literature and Douglas began to show him a New Testament which he seemed interested to receive. At that moment in this long stumbling conversation another stranger arrived at our door and came and sat beside his friend wanting to know what he was reading. The first man, embarrassed, abruptly gave back the New Testament and quickly left. We never saw them again. We wondered if one was spying on the other.

Later another man came to practice his English, or so we thought. "What is your name? Where do you come from? Do you like China? Do you like Chinese food?" "Yes" was our quick response. "Do you like baodzi?" He then followed with a long list of Chinese foods.

Enthusiastically Douglas answered "Yes" to every item. A couple of hours later we were ushered to the dining room and found our table loaded with all the delicacies we had apparently ordered! As our Chinese host stood with a smile of satisfaction, we were appalled at the amount before us and the protocol which required us to sample it all with due appreciation. We did our best, losing our appetite as we saw the stained table-cloth and the dirty floor with scraps of others' leftovers. We staggered back to our room, overstuffed and somewhat sick.

"One thing I know," said Douglas emphatically, "I am not going to eat another thing until we leave this train. I feel sick! Now I know what that man was doing. He was not practicing English — he was taking orders for our meal in the dining car."

Later, my upset stomach felt like what I needed was some soothing tea and toast. We were well prepared for our Chinese friend when he next appeared at the door. Painstakingly, holding his stomach tenderly for dramatic affect, Douglas soberly told the man, "Wo bing le!" which translates into "I am sick." He carefully explained as well as he could that he did not want to eat anything.

"But my wife" he went on, "she would like tea and toast." Tea was no problem to order. Douglas knew the word, "Tsai." But toast? He looked up his little English-Chinese dictionary and there was no word for "toast." Douglas proceeded to gesture, "Foreign bread. . .cut with a knife" as he sliced the imaginary loaf with his hand. "Then you heat it." The man smiled knowingly and off he went.

We were still recovering from our mild state of nausea when our Chinese host came back bearing two plates, each piled high with nine slices of thick bread fried and soaking in pork fat. Paled at the sight, we looked at this unwanted generosity and offered effusive but hypocritical thanks so as to save face for our friend. For the rest of our trip we tried to figure how to dispose of such a quantity of inedible food. We wanted to throw it out piece by piece but the window would not budge. Ultimately, we chose to drop some down the hole in the floor that served as a toilet and to hide some in our suitcase to get rid of when we got off the train.

It was ironic that we were struggling to discard food while, in nearby fields, the Chinese farmers we passed by on the train were working so hard to produce enough to survive. Day by day, they cultivated irregular sections of hillsides using animals and old-fashioned plows. Theirs was a life of strict economy, discipline and hard work. They had successfully overcome agricultural and political hardships to survive. That made the hardships of our journey seem quite small.

As our train journey came to an end, we prepared ourselves for the one day we had in Shanghai to make arrangements and leave for Hong Kong. *"Dear Lord,"* we prayed, *"You know we do not have any time to waste. Please help us get through all the red tape in this one day."*

In life's journeys we are often taken by surprise and we had no idea what was awaiting us. But the Lord had provided our tickets just in time and helped us on our way. We could trust Him to take us to our destination.

EXODUS FROM THE RED SEA — PART 3

At last, after chugging along for 26 hours, someone shouted the city of our destination— "Shanghai!" We had been carefully instructed to get off at the main Shanghai station where we would be informed how to proceed to the China Travel Service. We knew it needed to be a fast-paced, no-mistake day. We had to leave China that evening to have time enough to rendezvous with our Crossroads team in Hong Kong before we all flew to Korea.

Douglas and I got off the train and looked at each other in consternation. "This doesn't look right. This is not the famous railway station of Shanghai. Where have we landed? This has to be a substation," Douglas said. It turned out to be Shanghai West, about 20 miles from the main station.

We had barely stepped off before an official advanced towards us, asking for our passports. No one spoke English and we were ushered, like suspects, into a waiting room. We tried to signal our compliant cooperation by nodding with a smile and saying, "Shi, shi ni." We hoped our "Thank you" in their own language would encourage their support of our own plans for the day.

In a short while our passports were returned. By sign language and our few Chinese words we hoped we had conveyed our need to get to the main Shanghai station immediately. Courteously the officials put us in a taxi. We rode for miles in unrecognized territory. Douglas made me nervous with his remark, "I don't know Shanghai but I know we are not going in the right direction." My anxious thoughts turned toward the Lord, *Why, Lord, are we wasting time like this? Didn't we ask You to help us get through the day and all the red tape without delay?"*

Suddenly Douglas blurted out, "I know where we are! We have bypassed the main train station and here we are at the ticket office of the China Aviation Service. We have actually saved about two hours of time because we would have been directed here from the main train station." We arrived a minute or two before 9 a.m. when the office opened and were quickly served. *Oh Lord, Thank you. You are so faithful. You have got us here in perfect timing.*

We expressed our desire to get reservations on a plane to Hong Kong that evening. We had tickets but no reservations. Our visa was expiring at midnight. We had some "People's money" which would allow us to buy food, but very limited "Tourist money" needed for taxis, hotels and airline tickets. We were told all planes were booked until Saturday and that the plane only had first class space. We would have to pay $400 extra to make that reservation. We tried to impress the agent with the urgency of our request and then heard refrains which became the theme of the day: "Bu neng. Bu dui" meaning, "Impossible. Not permitted." We shared our dilemma with someone waiting his turn to buy a ticket and heard the same words, "That's impossible."

To our surprise the taxi was waiting for us so we asked him to take us to the Jin Jiang Hotel. Our last hope was to negotiate with the Cathay Pacific agency in this hotel. With relief we found the agent spoke fluent English and understood our problem quite clearly. But the news was just as bad. "We don't have any space. In fact, we have over booked and we have 25 standbys on our plane leaving tonight. There is no way you will get on this plane." My husband pleaded, "But our visa expires tonight, we have to get out of China." The quick response was, "I advise you to get your visa extended right away." We asked, "Where do you go for that?" He gave us an address. It was on the other side of the city.

At that moment a Canadian journalist overhearing our conversation, offered to help, "I'm going in that direction, why don't you come with me?" We were delighted to take the offer. In the car we were able to talk freely. We briefed him quickly on our situation. He commented, "In China you travel in tour groups or under escort, how is it the two of you are traveling by yourselves?" When we explained that we were missionaries, he exclaimed, "That explains it. Only missionaries could remain calm in your situation!"

We were dropped off at the Police Department for Foreigners just as the gate was being closed for the noon break. Douglas quickly put his foot in the way and squeezed us through to the office. We presented our request for an extension of our visa right away and the officer said, "Bu nung. Bu dui." He suggested we leave our passports and come back the next day. We pleaded help saying we needed the visa extended immediately. He went to talk to some superior official and gave us the good news, "Come back after lunch."

One might say we ate the "bread of adversity" for lunch as we had little appetite pondering the few options left open to us. We did not have enough tourist money to book into a hotel for even one night. We knew nobody in Shanghai. There was no Canadian Embassy in Shanghai. Though we had money in America and Canada, we had no way to access it. We felt strangely lonely in this big city crowded with people.

We picked up our visas after lunch and told the police that we wanted to report back to the Jin Jiang Hotel but didn't know how to get there. They suggested we go on the bus, but Douglas had doubts. He had been warned not to go on Shanghai buses. First, you don't know where they are going, because signs are in Chinese characters. Secondly, they twist and turn, and not knowing the route, you could lose all sense of direction. The police kindly took the time to write out our destination on a slip of paper and the bus driver delivered us safely to the hotel.

We went back to the Cathay Pacific Agency hoping that something might have happened to clear the way for us. "Nothing has changed" we were told, "I don't advise you to go to the International Airport with any hope of getting on this plane." Nevertheless, at our request he did put our names on the waiting list, numbers 26 and 27.

We felt desperate and desperately in need of prayer. We also began to face the probability that we were not going to get out of Shanghai and connect with our team in Hong Kong. Troubling thoughts rumbled in my mind, *Shouldn't we call our leaders in Hong Kong to ask for prayer? They need to know where we are and the crisis we are in.* A clerk assisted us in making the connection and we had a few moments of comfort talking to our YWAM leader there. "All we can tell you is that we are in Shanghai, without a way to leave, with no tourist money for a hotel, and no way to make money transactions." It was wonderfully reassuring to know that they would partner with us in prayer. We were not alone any longer.

At a later date we heard that the YWAM leaders in Hong Kong were in phone contact with Kona, Hawaii, and shared our need with them. The Crossroads class in Kona also agreed to pray for us.

After the brief respite of that telephone contact we sat down in the hotel lobby to rest. We felt stalemated. Helpless. Anxious *We have no place to go. Will we have to sleep on the street?* We both felt we could go no further. We needed to stop, to be still, to sit in the presence of the Lord.

"I think we need to listen to the voice of the Lord and ask Him to speak to us," one of us suggested to the other. After all the striving it was good to be quiet and ask the Lord what He wanted to say to us. We waited in silence. Listening. "I think He spoke the word 'Jehovah-Jireh' to me," said Douglas, "The Lord will provide."

"That's interesting," I said. "I seemed to hear 'I have helped you until now.'" It was a call for faith to trust a faithful God. Graciously, God stirred faith in us to fight the enemy of doubt around us, the words of others, "Impossible. Not permitted" and the enemy within us, unbelief.

With new confidence Douglas announced, "We are going to the International Airport as a statement of faith. We will use our last tourist money to get there by taxi!"

We spoke to the clerk at the Cathay Pacific desk and found we were the first standbys to arrive at the airport so we were listed number 1 and number 2. We were four hours ahead of flight time. Our euphoria at being numbers 1 and 2 on the list was soon challenged by a man from Singapore. In an angry voice he declared, "Why are you numbers 1 and 2? I should be first." Douglas quickly tried to soothe his ire, "That's no problem — we are trusting God to get us on that plane and He can provide three spaces as easily as two. You go as number 1 and we will be numbers 2 and 3!"

"Well, your God better come through" came the quick retort, "I have been waiting here since 8 o'clock yesterday morning. I want any plane that will take me out of China. If I don't get on this plane I'm going to Beijing and try to get out of the country from there!"

With hours to wait we had nothing else we could do but pray. Like a revelation we thought of the contrast between what we had been hearing all day, "Impossible" and what God's Word says, "With man this is impossible, but with God all things are possible" (Matthew 19:26). I found myself pacing in fervent prayer, my heart fearful at the circumstances but my spirit rising in faith. With all the confidence I could muster I told the Lord, "I am standing on Your promises and not on man's words. Lord, You say ALL THINGS ARE POSSIBLE with You (Matthew 19:26). I am standing on Your Word." I prayed stomping on the concrete floor to emphasize the solid foundation of God's truth which prevails against human words and thoughts.

After praying so earnestly a measure of peace and hope would lift my spirit until I saw bus loads of tourists arriving at the airport. Our hearts sank and our hopes began to fade at the sight. We could not believe any plane could carry so many people. Back I went to prayer, "But Lord, Your

Word says. . ." and I reminded Him of His promises. At one time a bus load of Greek tourists arrived at the airport and Douglas found himself talking in Greek to Greeks from Athens in the Shanghai International Airport!

Suddenly we heard an announcement over the loud speaker, "All standbys for the Cathay Pacific plane may go on." *What? Have we heard right? 27 people? How could that be?* My husband charged to the desk, asking, "What happened?" "A tour bus failed to show up," she explained, "we have forty extra seats!"

In all our lives we have never been rushed through red tape as we were at that time. They pushed us all through the various checks and paperwork, giving us five minutes to use up our last Chinese money at the tourist shop on our way to the plane.

We sat stunned, strapped in our seats. When the fancy menu arrived we concluded that God had even provided a celebration banquet complete with free champagne! We flew to Hong Kong feeling like V.I.P.'s or like Israelites escaping the Red Sea.

"Jehovah-Jireh and Ebenezer" was the motto of the China Inland Mission in which I grew up as a child. God gave me more than a sentimental journey. It was a spiritual journey — to prove once again His faithfulness as Jehovah-Jireh and Ebenezer and to the promises in His Word. These are the treasures of my spiritual heritage.

GOD'S CREATURES

As a missionary daughter I grew up with some knowledge of this life and the call of God to missions. Meeting missionaries, reading biographies and listening to missionary adventures, I developed a great respect for them. I felt in awe of the sacrifices they made: separation from families, financial challenges, dangers in some uncivilized cultures. And while I always wanted to be a faithful follower of Jesus, I secretly hoped that I would never be called to serve the Lord in the tropics with its hot climate and numerous creatures.

Ironically, that's exactly where we were headed.

As preparation to joining Youth With A Mission, we would spend three months in school in the very geographic locality I dreaded most – the tropics. It was a big change for us and I did find it wrenching to leave our home, family and home-ministries for this island in the Pacific. But my heart was to follow the Lord though I felt it ironic to be going to the very geographic locality I dreaded — the tropics.

One of our first nights on the YWAM base my husband lay in bed sound asleep while I relaxed by reading a book. Suddenly I was hit by something. *What was that? Could it be? Yes it probably was! A black creature. A flying cockroach?*

Where is it now? The awful realization made me shudder — a huge black cockroach hit my cheek. The shock was compounded by my husband who suddenly snapped out of his slumber and sat bolt upright in bed and shouted in alarm, "It's an earthquake! Yes, it really is an earthquake!" Quickly I hushed him attempting to calm his fear, "No, Doug, it's a huge cockroach. Go back to sleep!"

Our night life has included other intruders. One time I couldn't get to sleep and kept feeling little crawly things. *I have hit the pits. Am I feeling ants, bed-bugs, or fleas?* Then the feeling went away and I decided I was imagining it. *Perhaps I'm getting paranoid. . .or is there an evil presence in the room?* Douglas put his arms around his fidgety wife and we both tried to go back to sleep. I nearly dozed off when I felt it again. I definitely did feel a creature on my hair. I tried to jump out of bed but Douglas, feeling protective, kept clinging to me. I didn't want his arms right then—I wanted OUT! I commanded, "Let me go!" and quickly put on the light and there was the huge black cockroach (what locals call a Kona Cruiser). Douglas nobly dispatched it with the death blow of a fly swatter.

At some seasons we discover long trails of ants on pilgrimage across the walls of our kitchen or dining area. They race across our counters and on to us. Tiny as they are I have sometimes found it difficult to beat their speed to catch them. They are uncanny watchmen who race to plunder a piece of cheese or a drop of jam that might be left on the counter.

Another day I walked into the kitchen of our condo and there, hanging on the jar of pickled peaches not one foot away from where I stood, was a huge green gecko. It hugged the bottle, defied my proximity and wouldn't budge as if determined to claim its share of the contents. I remember the scene when Douglas with his kind heart opened the window, gently patting the creature in the direction of outside, saying tenderly, "There you go. . .There you go. . ." He used to catch a fly with a fast swing of his hand and open the door to let it fly away. My children used to quote the Proverb 12:10, "A righteous man regardeth the life of his beast: but the tender mercies of the wicked are cruel" (KJV). It was no guessing game as to which parent was "righteous" and which "wicked."

One morning I poured myself a second cup of coffee and out of the spout came a bleached dead gecko. *That's enough to make me sick. Just to think my first cup was brewed with a boiled gecko. Even in the Bible in Leviticus 11:29-30, geckos are listed as "unclean" animals.*

Another day I entertained Donna Jordan who with her husband founded a ministry called "YWAM Associates International." It networks with hundreds of thousands of YWAM alumni. When they left Kona, Donna felt the Lord told her to give away many of her possessions. She gave me a beautiful tray, with flowers and birds hand-painted by her mother. I decided to surprise her on this visit by serving a fancy ice cream sundae on this lovely tray. I was traipsing along when I suddenly noticed a big, fat, green gecko crawling down my arm. Squealing, I threw the tray on the sofa and poor Donna thought I had gone beserk. "It's just that I haven't yet learned to love all God's creatures. . ." I explained.

One of the delights of living in the tropics is exchanging an alarm clock for the songs of the birds. At certain seasons we also have a little drama when the brilliant red cardinals visit us. They come to our lanai (porch), and the lady cardinal sits waiting on the edge watching the male make a fool of himself. He flies into our mirrored wall and bangs into his reflection over and over again, wondering why that other bird doesn't give up. We dialogue in imagination, *Dear cardinal, you are your own worst enemy. . .Forget the competition. . .Don't get absorbed with your own self-image. . .You're fishing in the wrong pond.* My husband would suggest that he thought the lady was saying, "Hurry up and get this over with. As far as I can see, there is no difference between the two of you!"

God made all creatures, animal and human. Some appear to us as enemies, giants to be over-come and we jump around like grasshoppers in the face of these enemies.

Proverbs 30:24-28 exhorts us to learn wisdom from some of the animal activities, such as the diligent preparations of ants. Even lizards are mentioned as vulnerable yet living in the palaces of kings. As lowly in God's sight as a gecko is in ours, we shall one day live in the palace of the King of kings.

Now, after 14 years, I have learned a measure of coexisting with the geckos. They have had children and some of the babies even look cute to my eyes though, like human babies, we have to tolerate the droppings and stains they leave on our walls and on the clothes in our closet.

The other day I surprised myself by my reaction to two cardinals hopping around our living room. Previously I would have screamed for my husband to help get these flying creatures out of our small space. Instead, I found myself speaking to the birds in a sweet, gentle tone, "Out you go, darlings!"

The psalmist (148:7-10) calls for a universal chorus of praise to God including wild animals, small creatures and flying birds.

If God's heart desires "everything that has breath" (Psalm 150:6) to praise Him, surely it is not right for me to exclude these choir members.

RAINBOWS AND SUNSETS

I looked on the horizon and saw a cloud expanding in the sky – a cloud of communication technology covering the earth. I felt threatened and wanted to hide. Then a thought, like a ray of hope and sunshine burst into my mind, *Well, at least I can escape the need to learn computers. I'm not part of this generation that feels it needs them to function. I can get away with using the typewriter and my calligraphy pen. Actually, I'm closer to the quill pen era.*

When we joined the staff of Youth With A Mission on the Kona campus in 1985 my husband had a clear mandate — create a curriculum for the College of Humanities and International Studies. I dreamed that perhaps my role would be to dress in a muu muu and "talk story" to visitors, telling all about God's wonderful works and the history of the mission.

It didn't work out quite that way. The Business Administrator of the University's Accounting Department was looking to replace a staff member who was departing in just two weeks. "You are a detail-person, and we need someone for the Accounts Payable desk. Would you be willing to take that on?" It was like a burst of lightning, a shock that nearly struck me down. My thoughts raced with panic, *How could I possibly work in the Accounting Department? How absurd! I don't know how to use a calculator, let alone a computer. How could I take on the responsibility for printing all the mission support checks and all the vendor payment checks? Who can learn skills like that in two weeks? I'm totally unqualified. They must be desperate to even ask me.*

Then another thought dropped into my mind, *This is like stepping out to walk on water. I'm sure if I do step out, I'll sink, but, if Jesus is there, He'll keep me from drowning. That's what happened to Peter in the Bible. I'm supposed to be ready to say, "Yes, Lord" to whatever He asks me to do. But this? What a risk!*

In fear and trembling I agreed to step out and make the attempt.

I had a hands-on crash course in the Accounting Department trying to learn computers and procedures in two weeks. The stress made me break out in a rash and almost caused my patient mentor, Martin Rediger, to give up. But we all humbled ourselves and prayed for one another. God's grace for me and His patience and kindness in others brought us through that intense period.

In those four and a half years serving in the Accounting Department, my skill and speed improved remarkably and I came to love working there. Even in the pressure of work, we had many laughs and a good spirit in the department. One time I noticed that a single error could delay the whole check-run procedure for two hours. We were always working against a time pressure and so I reasoned, *If the Lord has given me the ability to do this operation with only one error, He can give me the ability to do it without any errors.* I walked outside the office and stood in a little niche unseen by the others, facing the Plaza of Nations, and cried to the Lord to give me 100% accuracy in my work. I do not recall making another mistake in that procedure and shortly afterwards, a new process circumvented that complicated delay.

At that time, we had one huge central mainframe computer in a special room in another building. One of the peaks of attainment was to learn the 25 steps to reboot the computers when they all went down. At one period the head of the Accounting Office and myself were the only ones on campus who knew this procedure, and I had a false sense of power when I heard this monster machine respond to my maneuvers with a roar. All computers were working again!

Our children converted my cloudy concern about computers into a rainbow of delights, bringing color and communication into our family circle. Not to be outdone by Mom who now could write home-letters on the computer, they began to regularly write to us on theirs. We have had much more communication than we ever did when we lived closer to one another and depended on visits and telephones.

The work in the Accounting Office was demanding and I spent many hours in overtime to meet the check deadlines. At times fatigue would set in and I longed to take a rest. One Sunday morning I could hardly face the effort of going to church and I asked my husband, "Douglas, would it be all right for me to stay home and not go to church this morning?" With kindness born of insight he wisely responded, "It's not only all right for you not to go to church, I order you to stay home." Those words not only lifted the burden of a guilty conscience but freed me to experience a serendipity.

I lay exhausted on the sofa that Sunday morning and felt a blend of fatigue and failure, unable to keep the pace and cope with the pressure of my ministry. But I lifted my heart to the Lord asking Him to speak to me. In that quiet moment I heard the word *"Covenant — remember My covenant."* Then the Scripture came to me:

> O Lord, God of Israel, there is no God
> like you in heaven above or on earth
> below — you who keep your
> COVENANT OF LOVE
> with your servants who continue
> wholeheartedly in your way.
> 1 Kings 8:23

I felt a sudden impulse to get up and look out toward the ocean. I saw a magnificent rainbow stretching from horizon to horizon in an awesome arc. *God's love covers us across the entire horizon of our lives and experiences. We may falter and even fail but He remains faithful in His love.*

We saw many beautiful rainbows in Hawaii. We have seen double rainbows. One time going up the side of a mountain we drove right through a rainbow. There was no pot of gold seen at the end of the rainbow but the glory of that experience still glitters in our memory.

A spectacular view occurred during a worship time watching the sunset with students from the School of Biblical Studies. With the students we scrambled over the lava rocks, Douglas carrying his Celtic harp. We sang with the sound of the mighty splash of surf on the rocks around us. We had been teaching the book of Revelation to the students. Together we marveled at the majesty and brilliance of the One sitting on the throne, set in brilliant colors with a rainbow encircling the throne, and heavenly beings all around (Revelation 4.)

We watched the sunset in silence and wonder. In awe we saw a globe of brilliant gold light amidst dark clouds and radiating pink rays, with clouds on either side, shaped like worshiping forms bowing towards it. A beautiful rainbow arched behind us. None of us had ever seen a sunset like it. It was a spectacular display of God's glory in creation, like a vision of heaven in the sky. We sat still in worship.

The rainbow was given as a sign of God's covenant — a sign of God's mercy and a promise of protection from a flood of judgment that would destroy the world.

Some days seem covered with clouds of darkness or confusion. When God's love shines through, the storm and rain are transformed into symbols of beauty. Rain needs rays to make a rainbow. A rainbow reminds us to remember the unbroken covenant of God's love in the past as well as the promise of His unfailing love for the future.

DEPORTED

In 1990, we joined several hundred YWAM leaders at Puerto Iguazu, Argentina, for an International Strategy Conference. The sessions were inspiring and challenging but we were all suffering in the 100-degree heat. Some leaders actually chose to conduct their business while cooling off in the swimming pool and others of us just wilted in weariness.

Our one escape from the heat was an outing to Iguazu Falls, on the border of Brazil and Argentina. As we stood only a few feet from the edge of the stupendous cataract, we felt humbled as Canadians. The height and volume of Iguazu Falls vastly surpassed the magnificent Niagara Falls, which we claimed as one of the seven wonders of the world.

As we watched the awesome grandeur of the Iguazu Falls we noticed an almost hidden scene. Clinging to the rock were a group of birds, secure in "holding on" together with the avalanche of water all around them. They were resting on wet, slippery rock, seemingly unaware of the proximity and enormous power of those falls to hurtle them to destruction. I believe God wants us to be at peace like that in the midst of life's swirling tempests, and the next part of our journey was a test of our faithfulness.

At the end of the main conference, our international leaders from the University of the Nations College of Humanities left by a sleeper-bus for meetings in Asuncion, Paraguay. We had no problem entering and leaving the small section of Brazil on the bus route to Paraguay. At the Paraguay immigration office, where we arrived about midnight, we were asked to pay a fee in either Brazilian or Paraguayan money, neither American or Argentinian currency would be acceptable. It so happened that Douglas and I had changed a fair amount of money into Brazilian funds and were able to bail out some of the YWAMers who might have been stranded. All passed the immigration inspection except us. We were told that with our Canadian passport we needed a visa, although we had previously checked and been told that visas were not necessary.

Some of the South American leaders argued with the officials as they negotiated on our behalf. YWAMers came off the bus and formed an outside circle of prayer while voices rose as the situation became more intense. "These people are old," our friends pleaded, "they are good people and they can't speak the language." *Are they wanting a bribe? Surely they won't leave us stranded at midnight in this deserted place?*

But that is what they did! The leaders, David Hamilton and Gerson Ribeiro, looked devastated as our bags were taken off the bus and we faced the prospect of going back alone to Brazil to get visas. Wedge Alman, who pioneered YWAM ministries in South America, kindly offered to accompany us as he was fluent in the language.

We started back to Brazil in a taxi around midnight and tried to find somewhere to stop for the night. After ten different places turned us down, the taxi driver indicated that he couldn't keep driving through the night. Wedge was using the opportunity to preach the gospel in Spanish to the taxi driver while we in the back were praying in English for a place to sleep. *Surely God doesn't expect us to spend the night with our baggage on the side of the road? And, O Lord, please help Wedge to witness effectively.*

At last, at 2:30 a.m., our 11th stop, we got accommodations in the Hotel Plaza and settled in for the short night.   The next morning we were amazed to discover that this hotel was around the corner and a block away from the Paraguay Embassy where we needed to go to start our visa process. *Lord, You know all things. How wonderfully you lead Your children!*

We were determined to overcome the temptation to get discouraged and to make this a day of prayer and spiritual warfare. However, we were quickly challenged when the Embassy also insisted we needed a visa which would include a Medical Certificate, two photographs and a return to Argentina to get our passports stamped for legal entry into Brazil.

As we walked the streets in 106 degree heat, we felt flushed and weak, but we determined to fight in faith. We mustered what strength we could to pray for the people and the nation. But we felt like limp, wilted soldiers unworthy to fight a flea, let alone a foe.

The Lord must realize the sacrifices made by our staff from Australia, Switzerland, England and America who have come to Paraguay for the Humanities College committee meetings. Douglas has all the minutes and agenda as International Dean. Surely the Lord knows the meetings can't go on without us? This affects the future of our College in the University of the Nations. Are we going to get our visas in time for these meetings?

We trudged on until we found a camera store, where they agreed to take our pictures without an appointment for the visa application. Then we walked on to the hospital to find a doctor for a medical checkup and certificate. We had some misgivings when the doctor led us into his office with furtive glances and hand signals, quickly closing the door behind us. He reached into his drawer and pulled out a prescription pad, wrote two or three sentences and charged us US$30. He did not ask one medical question or give us one medical test. But we got what amounted to the Medical Certificate.

Since Wedge Alman did not have his necessary papers to enter Brazil, he decided it would be wise for him to wait for us while we drove in a taxi to Argentina in order to re-enter Brazil legally. At the border the man at the gate looked puzzled and asked, "How long do you intend to stay in Argentina? A week? Two weeks? A month?" Douglas perplexed him further when he answered, "One minute. Uno minuto!" He shook his head at us foreigners and stamped our passports.

Now we ordered the taxi driver, with much hand-waving and body-language, to turn around on the other side and enter Brazil. He began to speed past the officer and we shouted, "No! NO!" so he backed up. Here we met two hippies who could speak Spanish and translated for us. The officer looked angry, not at us but at "those stupid Paraguayans" and banged his protest with the stamp on our passports.

When we reunited with Wedge back at the hotel we were ecstatic that the visa process had gone so well — it looked like we'd make it to Paraguay after all. We were all tired and hungry so we located a nice open-air restaurant to have lunch and relax. We had barely begun our sumptuous buffet when the sky suddenly got dark and a violent storm erupted. People vanished from the outside tables and the rain came like sheets blown horizontally. The power went out so we finished our meal by the light of kerosene lamps.

When we returned to the Paraguay Embassy they informed us, "You do not have multiple entry — only one time IN and then OUT!" That was fine with us! When we arrived at the bus depot we were surprised to meet David Boyd, our Chancellor at the U of N Kona campus. He too had been delayed on his way to Paraguay because of a passport issue, and we were delighted to be traveling together now.

This time the Brazilians at the Paraguay-Brazil border wanted a Customs Declaration. We no longer had one since this form had been collected the first time we passed this border the day before. The Federal police hassled us, refusing to give us another form to fill out. Our bus driver got upset at the delay and wanted to drive off and leave us to the mercy of taxis. David suggested I go back and wait in the bus, showing the driver our intent to continue with him.

In the meantime, knowing his own papers were not in order, Wedge had stayed on the bus, unnoticed, while all of us had got off to get our clearance to proceed. On my return Wedge told me that some official, peering into the bus, noticed him sitting there. Assuming he could not speak Spanish, the official hand signaled that Wedge needed to get his passport stamped. Wedge smiled benevolently and gave him a thumbs-up sign of compliance, but he didn't budge!

At one point we saw David and Douglas pop their heads outside the office windows looking for the police officers who had suddenly bolted out the door with guns drawn in response to some alarm. The officers finally returned to the scene driving an old Volkswagen Beetle on the sidewalk! Wedge and I were not bored as we waited in the bus, entertained by bureaucratic drama. The passports were stamped and we arrived in Asuncion after midnight.

We were welcomed like family the next morning. "When we had to leave you at the Paraguayan border, we felt we left part of our hearts with you," said one leader in a trembling voice. We all marveled at God's kindness in getting us to the conference on time. All the YWAM friends there saw this as the answer to their many prayers throughout that night and day.

In sharing our vision for the College of Humanities and International Studies expanding into Latin America we were given a gracious hearing. The leaders had been concerned that our travel difficulties might make us resentful of the local authorities. They were moved by seeing that we had no bitterness, only love, for them.

We thought we were going to have to use argument and persuasion to convince these South American leaders of the validity of our part of the University of the Nations' ministry on their continent. Instead, God bonded our hearts and bridged our differences by sharing His grace in a time of testing and prayer.

Mission accomplished by love.

HEAVEN CLOSE — BUT
NOT YET

I sat watching my husband across the breakfast table. *He looks so tired. What is going on? Teaching two full weeks on history is too much after teaching New Testament Greek for three months. Perhaps he can hold on for these last two days and then he must take a rest.*

Douglas had chosen not to go on our early morning walk to the pier that day to rest an extra hour. At the table he looked listless and I suggested he eat something. "It might make you feel better." He seemed to be looking at me intensely, pathetically reaching for reality or help. He was losing connection. His body swayed. I dashed to grab him as he collapsed on the floor.

Immediately I ran across the hall to get help. At such moments the decisions race in your mind. *Should we call the doctor? Should we call an ambulance? Should we go immediately to the hospital? Should we lift him up or let him lie on the floor, covered up or propped up?*

To my great relief Douglas came out of unconsciousness and was able to speak coherently. *Was it just a fainting spell, after all?* I wasn't taking any chances. I called the doctor's office and to my surprise they took my call rather casually. I was told that there were no appointments available but the doctor would squeeze Douglas in between two other patient visits later that day. Douglas faded in and out of alertness a couple of times before our son John and fellow YWAM staff member Richard Stein helped me get him to Dr. James' office.

I requested that the doctor see him immediately or give him a place to lie down. The doctor's schedule was so full that he only checked briefly in and out of the examining room. The initial tests did not indicate anything serious. Richard remained in the waiting room while John and I chatted with Douglas for an hour before he was given the checkup. "It could be a bit of flu," said the doctor, "but given your husband's high blood-pressure history, I do not like the sound of it. I like this guy and I want to keep him around. I'll take an EKG and then it's probably best to put him in hospital."

Since it looked like it might be a while before it was finished, I went out to the waiting room to tell Richard to go back to the campus. When I wanted to go back in with Douglas, the receptionist insisted I stay in the waiting room. *That's strange. I'm always allowed to be with him in the examining room.* It was also strange when John and Richard came back in and said that emergency vehicles were pulling up out back.

Dr. James called me in and said, "Now I know what is wrong. His heart stopped." Douglas's EKG had at first appeared normal so Dr. James moved on to other patients. The nurse happened to leave the EKG machine on after the test, and something prompted her to look back at the graph. It was a straight line! Full cardiac arrest. Immediately she called the doctor who started CPR and saved my husband's life.

Four men were working on my husband when I got in to see him. They were giving him

235

oxygen and an external pacemaker before the ambulance trip to the hospital.

We need prayer — now!

One of our students was on the campus switchboard when I called and immediately she called every department for prayer. They faxed Loren Cunningham in England, David Boyd our Chancellor in Germany, and Darlene Cunningham in Santiago, Chile. Who can describe the support of this bond of prayer?

When we arrived in the Intensive Care Unit at the hospital, Douglas said he felt fine! Our pastor and other YWAM friends came to visit and pray but the external pacemaker was having to "kick-in" too frequently. The order was given, "No more visitors!" The surgeon, Dr. Peebles, felt uncertain about relying on an external pacemaker through the night. He decided to put in an internal pacemaker. To prepare his patient for the emergency surgery, he said with confidence, "We have done over 100 of these and we haven't lost anyone yet."

"You lose them eventually!" was Douglas's retort.

The surgery was done under local anaesthesia. Douglas chatted with the surgeon during the hour in the operating room and returned cheerfully to the ICU. At this point I recalled occasions when Douglas had expected tender-loving-care for minor ailments from his private nurse whom he married. He would say, "Margaret, if I came home from the doctor with a notice that I had only two weeks to live, I think you would say, 'You should be ashamed of yourself!' I noticed him now bantering with the doctor so I decided to give him another chuckle with our private joke. I whispered in his ear, "Douglas, you should be ashamed of yourself!"

When we visited the hospital the next day Douglas told us that he woke up, not having any idea where he was. Moreover, the whole previous day was gone from his memory. The patient next to him had also had a near-death experience and had heard celestial choirs. Learning that he had clinically "died" several times the previous day, once in the doctor's office and four times in the ambulance, Douglas felt decidedly disappointed and deprived. "I never got a glimpse into heaven. I would have liked to check whether the instruments they play are citharas or harps!"

We didn't need harps to praise the Lord from our hearts as we reflected on the "happenings" of the previous day. The first collapse occurred at home at a time when YWAM neighbors were still around to give immediate help. The serious cardiac arrest occurred in the doctor's office. The EKG machine was left on and the nurse just happened to look around and notice the flat line within 40 seconds. The surgeon told us that it might be possible to restore a heart beat after two minutes, but the patient would be brain dead. Our son John had arrived on campus only a few days before and we could be together. An extended YWAM family, local and abroad, surrounded us in prayer. It was no wonder that I slipped into soothing sleep that first evening. I felt comforted, like a child being held in the loving arms of prayer.

On a later follow-up visit the doctor, recalling the narrow escape from death commented, "We've been lucky." I quickly replied, "I don't use that word. We call it Divine Providence."

The miracles of God are often seen in His timings. He watches over us and holds our lives in His Hands. We echo the words of the Psalmist:

"I trust in you, O Lord, My times are in Your Hands" (Psalm 31:15). In His competent Hands we gain the confidence to "Trust in Him at all times" (Psalm 62:8).

HARD WORDS

My husband, a natural linguist, thrived in the international environment of the University of the Nations campus in Kona, Hawaii. He quickly learned how to greet our foreign students in 40 different languages, and the students always broke into smiles. I hoped the words would rub off on me, but it was never that easy. I tried to learn some of the beautiful Hawaiian language, but its flowing vowels often left me tongue-twisted. I sang Hawaiian hymns in church but never with much understanding.

My own struggles with words gave me an empathy for other Asian and European students trying to learn to communicate in English. One day I thought it was time to give our Asian students in our English Language school a gift of encouragement. I suggested that if they learned these two or three words, all other words would be simple by comparison. *This should give a boost to their learning curve and give them courage to keep trying.* On the board I wrote the name of Hawaii's little six-inch state fish:

Humuhumunukunukuapua'a

Having mastered that word I told the students a story of our son John when he started into first grade. He was a quick learner and his older brother was helping him so he found school quite boring. In a day or two we got a call from the school psychologist, suggesting we have John tested for school placement. He had written a letter to his teacher something like this:

Dear Teacher:
I don't think I should be in this class. I already know this stuff.
P.S. The longist word in the English Language is antidisestablishmentarianism
Sincerely,
John Feaver

He was tested and promoted a grade in spite of misspelling the word "longist."

The students were fascinated with these unusual words and listened carefully as I shared what I thought were truly the hardest words in the English language to say. Two small words. *Forgive me.* And the next hardest words? *I forgive you.*

I told them about an incident I remembered when I learned that lesson. I was sitting at the table with our eight-year old son, Peter, who came home for lunch. Suddenly a loud crash from the living room made us rush to see what had happened. There by the fireplace was my beautiful crystal flower vase broken in pieces. Impulsively I shouted my furor at Patches, the cat, who raced up the stairs as I dashed after her screaming, "You <u>bad</u> cat! You <u>bad, bad</u> cat!"

Back at the table, all appetite gone, I tried to gulp down the meal. Peter, perhaps grateful that he was not the culprit, spoke up, "Mom, shouldn't you forgive when someone's done something wrong?" I couldn't argue that point, and I didn't dare be an example of disobedience to my child. Without much repentance I said, "Let's go" and we went looking for the cat. Finding her, I said rather coldly, "Patches, please forgive me."

That duty done, I sorrowfully returned to the table dialoguing with my distraught soul. *I never did like Patches. She may be the kids' pet but she is nothing but a pest to me. She dirties up the clean windows with her paws and leaves me to clean them up again. That vase was a priceless sentimental gift, an appreciation gift from our Pastor brought from Germany to thank us for caring for his children while he and his wife were gone. We'll never be able to replace that vase. We can't afford beautiful vases like that.*

My reverie of woe was abruptly broken by my son's rebuke, "Mom, doesn't it say in the Bible, 'In everything give thanks?'" Yes it does, and to make matters worse, that very text was hanging on the wall at the entrance of our house.

My temptation was to indulge in a pity-party of grief over a broken treasure. God looks for a right heart response, an inward treasure of much more value to Him. As Jonah 2:8 puts it, "Those who cling to worthless idols may forfeit the grace that could be theirs."

The grace to forgive and a lesson those students won't easily forget.

WINNERS AND LOSERS

Life seemed enough of a rat race without watching sweating and panting runners in the annual Ironman Triathlon race. Over 1,400 athletes from around the world come to Kona, Hawaii, each October to compete by swimming 2.4 miles, biking 112 miles and running 26.2 miles. My husband, eager to observe the event, somewhat shamed me into showing some sporting spirit. "Margaret, people come from long distances to watch these athletes and here we are so close we could almost see them from our lanai."

"Well," I thought aloud, "we have never stood at the finish line. That would be different. Let's see if we can get a place there." We both trotted off to join the crowd and were able to get seats within yards of the finish line at the pier.

There, spellbound, we gazed in wonder at these athletes, as they finished in varying degrees of exhaustion and exhilaration. We stayed for eight hours, without stopping to eat, transfixed by what we saw.

Some runners threw their hats in the air in jubilation at achieving their goal. Others held high their national flags, proud to represent their country. Fathers carried babies or ran with family members who joined them at the end to cross that line together. Many, worn out, fell into the arms of those greeting them and had to be supported as they limped to the aid stations. Others, disciplined to the end, turned around and bowed to the spectators in formal courtesy. Some, eager to beat the one ahead of them, sprinted past a runner just to grasp a few seconds of advantage. A few participants reached out to hold hands with their competitors, choosing to celebrate their mutual moment of triumph side by side.

One athlete zigzagged back and forth as if he were drunk. Several security guards positioned themselves around him to avoid the catastrophe of a well-meaning spectator breaking through to help him and thereby, disqualify him. He was disoriented with exhaustion and dehydration and we stared in dismay as he staggered aimlessly. Security guards threw water over him to keep him alert. Little by little he moved in a forward direction and we felt a corporate sigh of relief as he laboriously reached the line.

We gasped as one athlete collapsed only 20 yards from the finish line. *After coming this far, is he now going to miss the goal? This is a tragedy. I can't bear to see it.* In unison, the spectators called out to get his attention and motivate him to keep going. The whole crowd kept shouting with one focus — to rescue this athlete from failing the race. Slowly, he raised his head as if he were listening to the noise. *It looks as if he is wondering if we are really calling out to him. We must convince him.* Excitedly, in a crescendo of enthusiasm and hope, the crowd screamed louder and louder. We were united in an intense urge to see him finish the race.

He started to move. We watched in agony. He couldn't stand up. But he began crawling to the finish line on bloody hands and knees! I felt like collapsing in tears from the stress of striving with him as he inched his way those last 20 yards.

He made it!

The events of that day revealed a shift of values. The hero we admired most was not the first to finish the race. It was not the speed that impressed us but the spirit of perseverance. The psalmist reminds us that God's "pleasure is not in the strength of the horse, nor his delight in the legs of a man; the Lord delights in those who fear him, who put their hope in his unfailing love" (Psalm 147:10-11).

The writer in Hebrews 12:1 exhorts us to remove what hinders us in the race of life so that we can run with perseverance the race marked out for us. He also reminds us that we are surrounded by a great cloud of witnesses. We cannot see them but we know they are there.

Instinctively on that memorable day my heart exulted, *"Lord, thank You for all those who cheer us on, seen and unseen, who give us the courage to persevere to finish the race — even if we have to crawl."*

ADVENTURE ALONE

It was a privilege to have the leaders of the
YWAM base in Porto Velho, Brazil, coming to our
Kona campus in 1994 to take schools in our College
of Humanities and International Studies. It took
effort and negotiations to make this trip possible
for Braulia and Reinaldo Ribeiro.

One day these Brazilian leaders came to us
and shocked us with a surprise invitation. "Once a
year we have an annual conference in Porto Velho,
and we bring about 100 missionaries out of the
Amazon jungle for a time of teaching and spiritual
enrichment. We would like to invite you to be our
speakers this year." *What? We are not world-class
conference speakers. What could we say to those giants
of faith who risk their lives pioneering in the jungle? We
are not experts in cross-cultural insights, linguistics or
survival techniques for trail-blazers and pioneers. I am
an ordinary YWAM wife and mother and this is out of
my orbit of ministry.* We looked into the faces of
Braulia and Reinaldo and tried to dodge the issue
politely, "Thank you for your kind invitation,
but..uh..we will need to pray about it."

For several weeks the invitation lurked in
the back of my mind while I kept busy in the
school, hoping it would go away. Douglas, however, was quite challenged by the opportunity and
eager to accept it. *This reminds me of when we first
came to YWAM and the Lord spoke to me through Psalm*

32:8-9: "I will instruct you and teach you in the way you should go. . .Do not be like the horse or the mule, which have no understanding. . ." I felt that Douglas was the galloping horse eager to go and the Lord rebuked me for being the reluctant mule.

The day came when we had to face it head on; we were taking our Brazilian friends to the airport and we had to give them an answer. Early that morning Douglas and I each sat with our Bibles trying to listen to the "voice of the Lord." We read in the Scripture and sensed the Lord speaking to us. We were both disappointed. It was not what either of us wanted to hear.

Douglas read in 2 Samuel 21:17, "Then David's men swore to him, saying, 'Never again will you go out with us to battle, so that the lamp of Israel will not be extinguished.'" As King David was exhausted in battle and protected by his men, Douglas had a pacemaker and felt this was a warning to him not to go.

I read in 2 Corinthians 4:1, "Therefore, since through God's mercy we have this ministry, we do not lose heart." It spoke to my condition of timidity. *O Lord, you know I have lost heart from the moment this invitation came. What would I have to say compared to the outstanding speakers and missionary heroes they usually invite? But, if you're telling me to go, I'll go.* We sat silent and stunned, but we knew we had heard from the Lord.

We needed confirmation of this guidance and received it from the leaders of the campus. We also hesitantly called the family and asked our daughter how she would feel about her Mom traveling alone to Brazil. Her answer was another confirmation, "No, I wouldn't be appalled if you went alone!" All escape routes were shutting down and we began to move forward. A special challenge to Douglas was the thought of me getting lost along the way. My sense of direction has always been so poor that he diagnosed my condition as *Navigational Dyslexia*. It actually comforted me to think I might have such a "disease" and not just be stupid.

Our leaders and friends on the campus wished me well and gave their strong support through prayer. Family and friends elsewhere, including the Sisters of Mary, followed my itinerary with prayer. One granddaughter prayed that God would send an angel. There were about 14 plane changes throughout the trip with one overnight stop in the Manaus airport on my return. I felt that would be my most vulnerable situation. I would have to sit up all night in an open airport waiting for the next connection and unable to speak the Portuguese language. God sent two "angels" that time, the area Director of Wycliffe Bible Translators and his wife arrived at the airport booked for the same plane to Miami in the morning. We had six hours of sweet fellowship through the night while we waited.

My time in Porto Velho was a further discovery of God's faithfulness and grace when we dare to obey Him. There were some small tests. My baggage did not arrive with me. We had heard about rare occasions when pioneer missionaries, in order to be accepted in an unreached tribe, would go naked like the Indians. They would come up the Amazon river, dig a hole close to where they landed and hide their clothes to have them available when they departed. By contrast, here was I, without my suitcase, unable to take my clothes off! We were all grateful my baggage arrived a day or two later.

There were other physical challenges of the trip. The conference was held in an area considered the malaria capital of the world, but the Lord protected me from mosquitoes as well as from snakes and other jungle creatures. The biggest adjustment was living with jumping frogs in the kitchen of the guest home instead of the geckos we live with in Hawaii.

The theme of my week-long message was *The Grace of God*. In a teaching-testimony style of presentation I recounted Scriptures and personal stories of God's multi-faceted grace in salvation, generosity, service, healing, suffering and fellowship. As the week went on other invitations came to speak at a church in town, to a youth group, to a ladies' group, and to the Wycliffe staff. A local journalist aggressively approached me with charm and persuasion to do an interview on President Clinton's politics. I declined sensing that was not part of God's call.

One afternoon I overheard an animated discussion among the base leaders. Strong opinions were being argued with nearly volatile emotions. They decided I might have some wisdom in their controversy which centered around ministry policies. Should some present ministries be reduced due to lack of staff and resources? Should some schools be closed or the cows on base sold? Oher pressing issues were also mentioned.

I felt on the spot. *I don't have a prophetic word. I'm not an administrator here. Lord, help!* I was taken aback by my own boldness, "It seems you are spending all your time talking to each other instead of talking to God." With sheepish grins all around, they went to prayer and told me later that God had resolved the problems and their evening meeting was a special blessing.

This visit to Porto Velho is a highlight of my YWAM ministry years. I was humbled by the courage and sacrifice of these beloved YWAMers. I was moved by the close cooperation of adjacent missions working together. Wycliffe leaders told me how much they appreciated YWAM's gift of enthusiasm and willing workers serving in the hidden places of the forest. YWAMers shared their respect for Wycliffe workers' linguistic expertise and helpfulness in using their state-of-the-art computer equipment and planes to serve common goals. These front line missionaries won my heart and esteem. Their hospitality was as generous as their welcome. They opened their hearts to me and to the Lord.

The Lord encouraged me through the words of the leaders who invited us. "We usually invite well-known authors and missionaries to speak at our conference to help us in strategies of ministry. But this week God has spoken to us in a different way. He has shown us how much He loves us and cares for us personally. You have been a spiritual mother to us."

It will take a lifetime and beyond to fathom the faithfulness of God Who calls us and to experience His unlimited grace which staggers our imagination. On my journey, I never lost my way but I'm forever lost in the wonders of God's ways.

TREASURES IN THE ATTIC

Our Dutch Colonial house in Bethlehem had proudly worn its slate roof for 70 years. But it was wearing out. We tried to patch its holes with individual slates but to replace the whole roof would have only been possible at an exorbitant cost. Sadly, we realized we had to strip it and give this gracious home a modern roof of shingles.

Before the slate removal could begin, our walk-in attic, which stretched the length of the whole house, had to be prepared. Huge sheets of strong plastic were placed over all the boxes and paraphernalia to protect them from the showering slate and dust coming through the cracks.
This was done by kind friends who stepped in to help with the first part of preparation because we were away serving at the University of the Nations in Kona, Hawaii.

As the slates came off, our friends were appalled at the accumulation of slate dust in the attic. As they worked to clean it up, they had to put on face masks to protect themselves from the airborne pollution. Thankfully, the central section was mostly cleared when we returned from Hawaii, and we were determined to finish the job..

That attic contained the clutter of 42 years of marriage, along with school memorabilia. Yet we were getting the message Solomon spoke, "There is

a time to keep and a time to THROW AWAY!"
(Eccl.3:6).

Our children and grandchildren came to
help us attack the attic. I caved inside at the sight of
the thick layer of black slate dust covering everything under the eaves. It was hot and heavy work,
even our home vacuum-cleaner rebelled. We had
to get a special wet-dry vacuum cleaner to handle
the load. With despair we noticed the dirty dust
had shamelessly intruded into the 31 boxes, the
sacrosanct sanctuary of Douglas's classical books.
Each book had to be individually cleaned. My
weary and turbulent mind wondered, *Is this a
picture of sin? This black evil has penetrated every
corner, even boxes within boxes. It seems that nothing
has been spared its pollution.* At one moment of
despair I displayed a dirt-covered box to the family.
I expected them to share my disgust and resentment for this mess. The response of one of them
took me by surprise, "Mom, we don't see the dirt
because of the treasure inside."

Then I noticed the contrast. The grandchildren sprawled over the attic floor were reading old
comics and enjoying other treasures of the past:
photographs, letters, school reports and art work,
newspaper cuttings and old stuffed animals,
patched beyond recognition but still loved. Later
as we met in the livingroom we rolled in laughter
as notes or poems written in early school days were
read aloud. It was a unique family reunion, appre-
ciating both the humor and the significant roots of
our past.

We gave away or threw away a fair amount
of our stored "stuff" during that roofing job. Two
years later we realized we had to complete the task.
It was time to sell this house which for 15 years had
served as our family home and for 25 years, includ-

ing the ten years we had been in Hawaii, had been the meeting place of the Bethlehem Christian Fellowship. We spent hours in the attic or up and down the staircases, loaded with stuff. It was a monumental task to unpack boxes, sort out, repack, carry out. There were countless decisions to make: what was to be kept, what to be given to the family, what might be garage-saleable, what given to the Salvation Army, what donated with a sigh of relief to the trash.

Friends and family came to the rescue. Weary, at times we felt we reached a plateau in the process, procrastinating decisions of storage of the "treasures" we wanted to keep. The Valley of Decision came perilously close to the Valley of Depression.

Parting with artifacts from the attic was cathartic but also nostalgic. So many of our things were symbols of friends who had met in our home fellowship. We had varieties of vases which had contained gifts of flowers on numerous occasions; beautiful bone china cups and saucers looking worn from much use through the years; scrap books including a small portion of a silk parachute used by one of the seven American men who liberated the Weishien Japanese concentration camp where all my family and school friends had been interned during WWII; and many other mementos of our childhood, our children and our ministries.

Emotions of sadness, the end of an era, stirred in my soul, *I feel my heart is torn as if we're severing our precious connections with the past.*

Visiting a local church brought a unique comfort to us. When the pastor noticed us in the congregation he reminded the members that many there had their spiritual roots in our living room. Receiving the warm welcome and sharing with these friends later we realized that tangible symbols may pass but living memories are not lost. These, and others like them, were moving on in their own ministries and serving the Lord in many places.

Sometimes our hearts cling to treasures stored in attics. How much wiser to cherish real treasures stored in heaven (Matthew 6:20).

BLINDED BY FEARS
AND TEARS

Douglas accepted the challenge with enthusiasm. The University of the Nations leadership
wanted him to write a curriculum as a core course
for the College of Humanities and International
Studies. It was a unique opportunity to create a
biblical world view curriculum as a pioneer project
for a college not yet founded.

For two and a half years Douglas wrote and
studied until slowly the magnitude of his real task
dawned on him. With the honor of the title "Dean"
came the truth of his calling. He was to start the
College for which he was writing the curriculum.
He was Dean, Professor, Secretary, and Trash
Collector. His office was a desk in a room with five
others heading up their departments. One, on the
Worship Committee, practiced singing with his
guitar across the room for hours at a time.

God gave the inspiration of a theme for the
curriculum from Philippians 4:8 using his own
translation from the Greek: Whatever is True
included Philosophy and Science; whatever is
Noble would be Biography; whatever is Just involved Law, Economics and Political Science;
whatever is Lovely would be Music, Art and
Literature; whatever is of Good Report would be
History. Upon reflection Douglas saw these virtues

revealed the character of God. The centerpiece of the curriculum would be the Lord Jesus who perfectly reflected the character of God. Therefore, the goal of the Humanities Core Course would be the motto of the mission, *To Know God and Make Him Known.*

With the curriculum completed and the brochures printed, an awful awareness came upon us. *We have no students. We have no staff. We have no facilities. We have no finances. And we're supposed to launch this school out of a non-existent College of Humanities?*

We knew we had to rely on God. We ran to Him like desperate fools set for failure. Douglas's father was a successful Vice-President of Frigidaire in Canada who proved his competency by selling a refrigerator to an Eskimo. He looked at his son, lost in the Classics and the glories of the 5th Century B.C. and doubted whether he could support a family or "sell a pill to a dying man." Publicity, marketing, staff recruitment and fund-raising were not his gifts.

When we needed help most, God encouraged us by bringing Bob and Vicki Lichty, leaders from YWAM in Spain. They felt led to become prayer-partners with us and joined us weekly for a year to pray for the start of the school. Knowing our limitations we prayed with the intensity of those who know they have no confidence in themselves. Once an impressive list of speakers were scheduled, we prayed all the more earnestly that students would come to hear them. We dared to pray for ten and eventually God gave us nine and another student part-time.

We learned that one student from France did not have his student fees but he was accepted "by faith." Our faith did not stretch for the awful truth revealed at registration. All nine full-time students lacked funds. Douglas and I commiserated with one another, *Does this mean that we are going to have to pay their deficits? Will we have to mortgage our house in Bethlehem which only was paid off the month before we left to come to this mission?* No! God will provide! And by the end of the school all nine students had their fees paid.

Other schools were added to the College in time: Hebrew, Greek, Teaching English to Speakers of Other Languages (TESOL), English as a Second Language (ESL) and English Language and Culture (ELC).

Each year, especially in the TESOL and ESL/ELC schools we were tested by the uncertainty of finding leaders and staff. Again and again we wondered if the deadline would pass, if the school could go on. Many times it was just "in time" that a teacher would agree to come. I pondered, *Now I understand why the Lord instructed his disciples to pray that the Lord of the harvest would send laborers into his harvest. I never realized the need and difficulty of getting "laborers." We are not gifted in recruiting but He has the authority to call and compel people to come and help in His work.*

In the late 1990s we prayed fervently for God's chosen person to take over the leadership of the College of Humanities as it was time for Douglas to pass on his role of Dean. Leaders of the mission were looking around the world and once again we were taken by surprise. God's wonderful answer was right here in our midst! It was a costly commitment for Robert Evans and his wife, Bev, but we were all encouraged when they gave their willing, "Yes, Lord."

Almost immediately we faced a severe test. We were within a month of the ESL/ELC Fall school, with a class of students and not one staff. Robert in his new role of leadership, supported by Douglas and myself, prayed desperately to the Lord. We made phone calls to former staff in distant places asking them if they could come over and help us. None felt called or able to help. Anxiously we thought, *How late can we leave it? We're going to have to cancel this school. It's not fair to the students coming from Korea to be told in the last month that the school is canceled because we have no school leader or staff.*

The deadline was reached with a sense of failure. *Why hasn't God answered our prayers as before? We long to pass on not only the leadership but the blessing God has granted to us in answered prayer all these years.*

Depressed and weary, with head bowed, an unwanted thought came into my mind, *What about you?* I felt like the little lad with his loaves and fishes in reverse — an oldie offering almost empty hands but a heart desiring to be made willing. More than ever we cried, "Help, Lord!" Yet there was a strange peace in our hearts as my husband, Robert and I decided to step into the gap. I, with no experience, would be lead teacher. Robert would be School Leader. Douglas, adept at languages would also teach English without any TESOL training.

A few days later Douglas and I were hosting the guests at the reception following the Friday night campus meeting. After a tiring week, we served only because we had committed to do so. We were relieved when the evening was almost over. Our attitude did not deserve any favor of the Lord yet He held a surprise for us.

Just as we were ready to close down at 10 p.m., a young couple from Canada happened to walk in. They were on four months sabbatical from their university teaching positions in Canada in the fields of computers and TESOL/ESL! They asked what they could do in some volunteer capacity on the campus. We were stunned. God clearly caused our paths to cross. They were already qualified as staff, having completed a Discipleship Training School seven years before. The wife graciously accepted the role of the school's lead teacher of the ESL/ELC school and mentored others who joined us on the staff.

I think of Hagar with her son Ishmael evicted by Sarah from Abraham's home. She wandered in the desert and finally, her water supply gone, sat down and sobbed. She put her son some distance away because she could not bear to see him die of thirst and dehydration. An angel of God from heaven spoke to her, "Do not be afraid." Then God opened her eyes and she saw a well of water (Genesis 21).

Sometimes the pool of tears in our eyes as we wail in prayer may blind us from seeing God's provision close at hand. In mercy He wipes our tears, opens our eyes and shows us Who He is. We behold a God who forgives our unbelief, loves us, cares for us and answers our cries.

LEARNING TO WALK AGAIN — A CRISIS
The Comfort of God's Love

My father often liked to describe my first wobbly steps crossing the courtyard in Lanchow, Kansu, China, where I was born. The delight of that memory stayed with him until he went to heaven the day after his 99th birthday in 1993. An early faded photograph shows him dressed in a Chinese gown with his arms outstretched to welcome his stumbling baby daughter in triumph.

Seventy-five years later my Heavenly Father stretched out His arms to welcome me as I struggled with wobbly steps. I had to learn to walk again after a serious injury to my ankle.

On the evening of November 22, 1999, I went out to mail the family home-letters. I was in no hurry. The evening was quiet and I looked forward to a prayer-stroll on the parking lot. But I missed a step and slipped on a wet landing and called out for help. People gathered around me, as I lay with my foot twisted under me in throbbing pain. While waiting for the ambulance, some Korean friends sat on the steps with me, moaning in sympathy. Strangely, their feeling my pain was a comfort to me. Others, some strangers, stopped to pray for me.

The ambulance men were gentle and kind. The one attending me was not only a Christian but knew our son John from the worship team of Holualoa Church. I felt a special comfort to be cared for by this previously unknown brother in our Christian family.

In the Emergency Room one attendant, looking at my bent ankle and the degree of distortion, exploded, "They're going to have fun X-raying that!" By 3 a.m., about six hours after the fall, I was settled in the Intensive Care Unit, having had many X-rays, oxygen, needles, blood pressure readings, medical histories and forms to sign. The surgeon also attempted to straighten the dislocated ankle under local anaesthesia. In the ICU the nurses apologized for the short night left for rest but they continued the frequent interruptions nonetheless.

When the anaesthetist came in the morning to explain the procedures of the spinal, the IV medication and the general anesthesia, she overheard the prayers of my husband and a friend who were visiting me before surgery. She looked pleased and said, "We need prayer, too." The male attendant who wheeled me into the operating room sang religious songs and quoted Scripture as we went along the corridors! My thoughts rose up in praise, *O Lord! Your Presence is with me and I am surrounded by those who also know and love You. I feel safe and secure. Thank You for Your care.*

How would I describe the three-hour operation? Bliss! I chose the music to listen to by ear-phones, and I have no memory of pain nor post-operative nausea on waking up in the recovery room.

My roommate, Sarah Kaupiko, was a dear 92-year-old Hawaiian saint who sang, *"For God so loved the world He gave His only Son..."* at any time of day or night. She had a nice voice and a cute chuckle and chatted incessantly. She "talked story" about the early Hawaiian days which fascinated me in spite of my half-doped state.

Sarah would call out to the nurse, "Girlie! Girlie!" and if no one came immediately she would say benignly, "Walaau! Walaau!" This interpreted is, "Talkity! Talkity!" Her cheerful spirit charmed us all, creating a sweet fragrance of the Lord she loved. The Lord's Presence was in that room. I felt at home.

Thanksgiving Day came two days after surgery. My spirit was thankful but I had no appetite for food. In a tender touch God sent me a special gift that day. A young family with two sons took time out of their holiday to visit me. These boys came to my side and prayed with such concern, I was deeply moved.

I know the Lord hears the prayers of these His little ones. My own faith is strengthened. My stomach rejected the turkey on the tray, but my soul was restored by the love of these children. *Lord, You can provide a table in the wilderness and set a Thanksgiving feast in a hospital room.*

My surgeon, Dr. Barry Blum, a gifted man with artistic and intellectual interests, shook my hand saying, "We're friends now, aren't we?" *Does he want to be sure that I have forgiven him for all his carpentry work on my bones? Or is he proud and pleased with the repair he has made?* That day when he looked at his work through my X-ray, viewing the line-up of eight screws and a metal plate for three fractures and a dislocation, he exclaimed, "Lovely!" He was into drama and theater, painting, music, history and medical "art!"

A call came from Audra Baumgarth, the wife of a licensed physiotherapist, offering their help. "Margaret, this is no light offer. We are serious and sincere." *Oh, they're so kind, but how can they possibly be of help? Audra has been in a wheelchair herself for years, a result of polio. Still, I'm touched by their offer.*

Weak and hopping with a cast and a walker, I dreaded the day of discharge, four days after surgery. Climbing 16 steps to our condominium was like facing Mount Everest. Never did I dream how much I needed the help of these dear friends. Not only did Audra's husband, Lee, come to the hospital to help me get home safely, but continued months of daily and then weekly visits to teach me to walk again. His wife cheered me on and sacrificed her time with her husband on these occasions so he could help me. She even loaned her own wheelchair so that I could participate in special events.

Our children decided together that Ruth, our daughter, should come to Kona and help. Her coming brought cheer and encouragement, a blessing to both her parents.

For three months, largely confined to our condo, I was withdrawn from the active life of campus ministry. God's words in Hosea spoke to my heart: "I will lead her in the desert. . ." (Hosea 2:14-16).

Is this a <u>desert</u> into which He has led me? If so, this desert is blossoming like the rose! I'm surrounded with so many flowers and plants and though I can't get around outside, many are visiting me. Why did this happen to me? What does God want to say to me?

In Hosea God goes on to say that He will "speak tenderly to her." *Oh, thank You Lord, if I've done something wrong and You want to rebuke me, You will not scold me harshly. You will speak tenderly. Is this the end of serving You in this place? I can't get around well with this major injury.*

Hosea continues God's words, "There I will give her back her vineyards and make the Valley of Achor (trouble) a door of hope."

Thank You, Lord, there is hope. But how shall I serve You?

God's answer is revealed in Hosea's quote, "In that day you will call me 'my husband;' you will no longer call me 'my master.'"

In the crisis I was awakened to the love of the Heavenly Father for a fallen child. I was lifted up and held tenderly by His lavish love expressed through those who prayed, wrote, visited, and showed kindness generously. I echoed the psalmist's words: "When I said, 'My foot is slipping,' your love, O Lord, supported me" (Psalm 94:18).

In a crisis we discover the support and comfort of God's love. His first desire is to assure us of His love and restore our first love for Him. We love to serve and work for Him. He may be pleased with the work of our hands, but he longs for the love of our hearts. His highest call is not to work, but to walk in love with Him.

LEARNING TO WALK AGAIN — CONVALESCENCE
The Discipline of God's Love

There is something noble and courageous about the kings of Judah who brought significant reform to a nation who had backslidden from the ways of God. Just as they are about to end their reign in glory, there's a change of heart in some of them or a foolish choice made and the story ends in disillusionment. The tragedy is a haunting warning to us as we get older.

King Asa was one who prayed a profound public prayer, "Lord, there is no one like you to help the powerless against the mighty. Help us, O Lord our God, for we rely on you. . ." (2 Chronicles 14:11). With God's help he faced a vast army and prevailed. He initiated a grand national reformation. It was said of him, "Asa's heart was fully committed to the Lord, all his life (2 Chronicles 15:17)." The tragedy of his life occurred two years before his death. He stopped relying on the Lord; he sought an alliance in a national crisis and relied only on physicians in a personal crisis — a disease in his feet.

In the months of convalescence while my ankle bones, muscles, ligaments and tendons were healing both from the accident and from major surgery the Lord had many things to say to me. I wanted to listen to His wisdom and learn from the warnings of those who served God well, but failed in their personal crises, often toward the end of their lives.

Convalescence demands more grace than a crisis. In sudden tragedy or accident we instinctively feel our helplessness and cry out to God. Coping with the consequences requires wisdom for daily decisions and patience for slow recovery.

As soon as I was discharged from the hospital Lee Baumgarth, my kind friend and physiotherapist, began training me to go up and down stairs, one step at a time, with a crutch or cane, hopping on one leg. At first I panted under the effort, broke out in a sweat, never sure that I had the strength or stability to make that hop up or down. I had lost confidence and feared falling again. Though I dreaded this daily ordeal, I also felt grateful for this necessary help.

I developed a confidence in my trainer, feeling safe in his care. My security was assured by staying close to my friend who held tightly to a belt around my waist. If I slipped, his strong hand would hold me up. As people passed by I mused, *I know I look ridiculous, just like a pet dog on a leash. But I don't care how I look. Lord, are you showing me that our security in life is walking closely beside you, not taking our hands out of yours?*

On one follow-up visit to the surgeon I asked, "Why am I so weak and tired? I have so little energy and now, I'm running a low fever. I don't have a disease, all I have are broken bones and injured soft tissues." His answer was revealing, "You have had a major injury. When a part of the body is hurt, the rest of the body sends its resources to that area for healing. All the systems give their strength to the suffering part and, therefore, even your brain is depleted in order to assist healing for the ankle." *That reminds me of the words of Paul, "If one part suffers, every part suffers with it"* (1 Corinthians 12:26). *That describes also the compassion and kindness shared by others who have suffered with me. We are called to share in each other's suffering and help in each other's healing. Those who do are like human angels with healing in their wings.*

After two and a half months the surgeon declared, "You are healed — but this is when the work begins if you are ever going to walk better than you can right now." The enemy of discouragement groaned in my ear. *Healed? With my foot so swollen that I can't put the same size of shoes on? I'm still limping in discomfort. Work? Haven't I been working hard all along, exercising and hopping up and down 70 steps at a time? Is all this worth the effort?*

I knew in my heart that I didn't want to spend the rest of my life anchored by an ankle or loping like a kangaroo at the pace of a snail. I signed up for a new intensive level of work at the Hawaii Rehabilitation Service for months more of massage, stretching and strengthening exercises using a variety of machines.

The bones were healed but ankle movement was limited and the challenge of this phase was to overcome discouragement with patience. Every session with the physiotherapist included constant corrections and instructions. I tried but my foot wouldn't follow my mental commands. *I'm telling my foot to bend inwards but it won't! This is like Paul's dilemma, "I have the desire to do what is good, but I cannot carry it out"* (Romans 7:18).

As much as I detested the thought, it looked as if I was going to have to walk with a cane. The challenge of learning to walk properly was compounded by the therapist's assessment that I had not been walking correctly all my life. Along with soft tissues injured through the fall and surgery, I had to break a habit of over 70 years. The effort wearied me and progress was slow.

Then the Lord reminded me of His love. Do not lose heart. . .the Lord disciplines those he loves. . .endure hardship as discipline. . .no discipline seems pleasant at the time, but painful. Later on, however, it produces a harvest of "righteousness" and peace for those who have been trained by it. . .Strengthen your weak knees. . ..make level paths for your feet, so that the lame may not be disabled, but rather healed (Hebrews 12:5-13).

With renewed resolve I kept up the relentless exercising, pushing against my comfort zone. One restless night about two o'clock in the morning I determined to get my feet to walk as they should. I repeated the instructions over and over with each step: "Take a smaller step with the left foot than the right; lean the foot inwards; bend the ankle as the right foot goes forward; bend the knee, don't hold it stiff; keep the hip joint in, don't compensate by swerving outwards." It took concentration and tears to break this habit of a lifetime.

All was not drudgery. The therapist also gave good doses of encouragement for any improvement observed. One day she asked me to lie down on the large bed to do some exercises. Next I heard her ask another patient with an injured ankle to lie down on the same bed. He looked slightly puzzled, perhaps perplexed or reluctant, but he obeyed orders. As I lay there beside this young male Hawaiian ambulance paramedic, a quote from the past flashed through my mind. I spoke out for all to hear, "Misery maketh strange bedfellows!"

A cheerful heart and a chuckle makes merry medicine.

Eventually progress was discernible, but one hurdle remained. I could go upstairs but not downstairs. A special four-inch stool was made for me to practice this maneuver, but my ankle would not bend. After months of work, I still could not do it. I felt utterly defeated and tempted to despair. I broke down in tears of frustration. I dialogued with my weary thoughts: *It only makes me feel worse to be defeated by such a small hurdle. I've come to the end of my resources. Not the doctors, nor the physiotherapists, not the exercises, medications or treatments have the power to give me the movement and healing I need.* My anguish seemed to be heard in heaven for a flash of revelation came to me: *You will have to rely on the Lord — just like King Asa did during his reign when God prospered him. What is impossible to you is possible with God.*

My acceptance of this truth was put to the test. The physiotherapist took me to some outside steps and told me to stand in the center at the top of the stairs. She stood at the bottom of five or six steps and told me to walk down those steps toward her, without holding on to a railing, a cane or a human hand. It was a hard and scary moment of decision. She assured me I would not fall. Could I trust her word? Only trust could overcome the feeling of terror. I could not trust myself, but yes, I could trust her.

In a leap of faith I did it! And my spirit leaped with triumphant joy.

She rewarded me that day with words I'd been longing to hear, "Now you can walk without the cane." I was thrilled, *No more cane! I can throw the cane away!*

In a crisis we discover the comfort of God's love In convalescence we learn about the discipline of God's love. We have a choice. We can limp through life with the comfort of a self-chosen crutch or we can walk with God, trusting and leaning on His love and power.

OUR GOLDEN JUBILEE

Looking back over 50 years of marriage, memories filled my mind and a mix of emotions stirred in my heart. Scanning half a century, there were both highlights and disasters we never dreamed would happen. I started out single, then entered marriage and now have a large family circle including children, spouses and grandchildren. I still think of our two children who died early. But God's comfort has always been with us, knowing those little ones had already spanned the space between earth and heaven. Another surprise of our lives is the amount of travel we've done in our 50 years together. We could not count the miles we have traveled together by land and sea and air in our 50-year journey.

We pondered, *How can we celebrate such a milestone of God's goodness and faithfulness? How can we bring honor to Him? The magnitude of the challenge paralyzes all planning.* In the end, Douglas and I decided that perhaps a private family dinner would be our best choice.

But our children chose to obey the fifth commandment and honor their parents, even though it meant breaking the eighth commandment to steal our address book. They sent out more than 700 invitations to come to a service and reception and to write a few words, a memory, a Scripture or send pictures to put in a Book of Memories as a gift. They huddled together as a committee of siblings and planned surprises. When the moment of reckoning came, they decided to donate their tax refunds to finance this once-in-a-lifetime occasion.

Little leaks of these secrets began to trickle into our ears or hands. We received beautiful cards and gifts in the mail. A former YWAM couple now in California were visiting in New York and stopped by to visit us in Bethlehem, Pennsylvania, leaving us a 50th wedding anniversary card. A friend in Florida phoned, "This is my gift to you because, if I came to your reception, I'd only get to give you a hug and this way I can talk with you for half an hour!"

Another leak revealed that my sister Doris, our maid-of-honor, was coming from Toronto by train, but Douglas still didn't know that his sister Dorothy, our bridesmaid, was flying in from Florida. Our daughter Ruth thought up a plan to surprise her father at the airport, "Let's suggest that Dad's carry-on case could be repaired at the airport, and we'll make that one of our stops on a bunch of errands." I carried on the intrigue in the minivan, warning that our Kona airport repairs had not been that good, but at least the job would get done. Douglas carried his empty case and had some trouble with the security check due to his pacemaker. Finally, the officials, checking and double-checking, freed him to proceed with a cheerful, "Have a good trip!" Douglas, ever honest, offered an unnecessary explanation, "I'm not going on a trip, I'm going to get my case repaired." Hastily I pushed him to keep moving on when he looked up and his face lit up with an incredulous smile of recognition, "Dorothy!"

So began the sweet rhythm of family re-unions and celebrations, non-stop talking and reminiscing in the joy of being together again. We'll capture one scene from those days. Three-year old Ben held up a bag of popcorn for his mother to pop for him in the microwave. Her response was, "You don't need a whole bag to yourself. You can share your brother's popcorn." Ben's retort, "I don't want to share." Auntie Dorothy picked up the cause, saying, "In the Bible it says to be kind and share." Ben was unimpressed. He stood upright before her, holding the bag in front of her as if he were holding an Old Testament manuscript, and said, "See! It says **DO NOT SHARE!**"

The anniversary service in the First Presbyterian Church sanctuary preceding the reception was a recapture of our wedding service fifty years before. The grandchildren passed out programs to the guests. We wore petite yellow/gold roses in the corsage and boutonniere. And with the lovely orchid leis sent from Hawaii, we felt double-decorated.

Our Church organist, Greg Funfgeld, famous as the Director of the Bach Choir, delighted us with his improvisation of a hymn. Douglas used to play this hymn, *"Turn Back O man, forswear thy foolish ways"* when, as a bachelor, he played the organ at weddings, much to the chagrin of his sisters. We could almost hear the man turning back with the deep, descending notes of the organ! The original processional, solo of praise and song of prayer, all composed and written by Douglas, were deeply moving to hear. The closing hymn of remembrance was one he wrote and composed for the Church's centennial celebration with the words so applicable to this occasion:

> *The flame of the Spirit passed down through the years,*
> *From candle to candle in new flames appears;*
> *From father and mother to daughter and son,*
> *As flame touches flame so the True Light goes on*

.

The service featured two prominent pastors in our lives. Keith Brown, our Presbyterian pastor, and Doug Seidel who represented our home fellowship ministry. Doug Seidel, in respect for my husband's taste for the classical languages, read the Scripture from Jeremiah 32:38-41 from the Septuagint version in Greek. Then he recalled to the congregation that at our Saturday night home meetings we carefully warned that when people spoke in tongues, the message was to be interpreted. Thus he obediently read this passage, which includes our marriage motto, in English!

"I will give them one heart and one way, that they may fear me forever, for the good of them, and of their children after them" (Jeremiah 32:39, KJV).

Pastor Keith Brown spoke with encouragement on the riches we have of "every spiritual blessing in Christ (Ephesians 1:3.) He shared the secret he had observed which was that we were not only wedded together but also to Christ. Then he declared, "The groom may now kiss his bride!" While laughter rippled among the observers, we joyfully obeyed with a hearty embrace and a loving kiss. As planned, at the close of the service, the pastor guided us to the reception area in this huge church. Again the audience chuckled. I was parading down the aisle on Keith's arm instead of my husband's!

The reception was an overwhelming experience. We stood for over an hour greeting and embracing friends from various eras of our lives: China childhood, WWII Air Force, Johns Hopkins University, Yale University, Lehigh University and University of the Nations. Thoughtfully, the guests wore name-tags to help us identify their faces! There were friends from a variety of churches: Evangelical Free, Baptist, Methodist, Assembly of God, Presbyterian, Roman Catholic, Greek Orthodox, Russian Orthodox and others.

Each of our dear children honored us with speeches, blends of POMES (not up to the literary standard to be dignified as a POEM) and stories, serious and humorous. John's pome is an example:

> *A thousand years are a day*
> *In God's sight, as the Bible does say.*
> *If a day with each other*
> *Is just like another —*
> *Charge on, and you'll reach Y3K!*

A love-song Douglas composed for our wedding reception was never sung by his sister Marianne. A signal given was misunderstood and she was not asked to sing. But she made a tape back then and at last we all heard it, at this reception, fifty years later! The family gathered around the piano and sang for those assembled our family grace, a round composed by Douglas, *Come ye Christians, join with me. Sing His praise in harmony. Hallelujah.*

After the last guest had left we went home and packed our bags for a family reunion at Camp Hebron. There we had time to relax, play games, rock-climb, do sports, take walks, go for a horse and wagon ride, laugh and talk together. Our theme for the family circle was *The Year of Jubilee*. We were to consider in our sharing time what ways we were to release people, such as forgiving people, or to report on a new freedom or restoration in some aspect of our lives. As always, our contributions bring forth confessions and chuckles as we covenant to pray for one another through the year.

The time came to return to Hawaii. We flew high in the friendly skies of United Airlines, our spirits soaring until we landed in Chicago and then in Los Angeles with the news that the flight to Kona was cancelled. Jet-lagged and weary, we stood in line for over two hours at the Los Angeles airport Customer Service counter. By the time we talked to someone, there were no flights left. We were transferred to a TWA flight several days later and given vouchers to stay in a hotel for three days and three nights. We had fancy buffet meals and a lovely room with a spectacular view as guests of the United Airlines. With rest and reflection we repented of our complaining spirit in the midst of airport chaos, realizing that all the time God had a surprise plan for us — the gift of a Jubilee Honeymoon at the Hilton.

We brought back with us our beautiful Book of Memories, which was presented to us at the reception. There were stories we could not recall involving incidents which the writers said had been life-changing: a small kindness, a telephone call, a Scripture or a prayer. Some brought laughter. Some moved us to tears. These were emails and letters from around the world. We were reminded of the prophet Zechariah's warning, "Who despises the day of small things?" (Zechariah 4:10). In God's service He can make the small significant.

As we perused this book of treasured memories spanning 50 years of life together we pondered on all the blessings of those years which were but the expressions of God's goodness and faithfulness to us.

The prophet in Malachi 3:16 tells us:

Then those who feared the Lord talked with each other,
And the Lord listened and heard.
A scroll of remembrance was written in his presence
Concerning those who feared the Lord and honored His Name.

If a book of memories can bring such joy on earth, what will that scroll of remembrance in heaven be like at our Grand Reunion up there?

My Prayer For You

Now I commit you to God and to the Word of His grace,
which can build you up and give you an inheritance
(Acts 20:32).

Breinigsville, PA USA
08 November 2009
227165BV00001B/1/A